T0100479

Data Curious

Applying Agile Analytics for Better Business Decisions

Carl Allchin and Sarah Nabelsi

Beijing · Boston · Farnham · Sebastopol · Tokyo

Data Curious

by Carl Allchin and Sarah Nabelsi

Copyright © 2023 O'Reilly Media, Inc. All rights reserved.

Published by O'Reilly Media, Inc., 1005 Gravenstein Highway North, Sebastopol, CA 95472.

O'Reilly books may be purchased for educational, business, or sales promotional use. Online editions are also available for most titles (*http://oreilly.com*). For more information, contact our corporate/institutional sales department: 800-998-9938 or *corporate@oreilly.com*.

Acquisitions Editor: Michelle Smith	**Indexer:** nSight, Inc.
Development Editor: Gary O'Brien	**Interior Designer:** David Futato
Production Editor: Ashley Stussy	**Cover Designer:** Susan Thompson
Copyeditor: Liz Wheeler	**Illustrator:** Kate Dullea
Proofreader: Kim Wimpsett	

July 2023: First Edition

Revision History for the First Edition

2023-07-14: First Release

See *http://oreilly.com/catalog/errata.csp?isbn=9781098143831* for release details.

978-1-098-14383-1

[LSI]

Contents

Preface

For as long as education has existed, there has been a focus on verbal and written communication. One aspect of communication in the 21st century has, sadly, not been taught properly: data management. Many people feel naive when it comes to working with data, due to this lack of education. No one likes feeling that they are asking potentially stupid questions, especially when people are looking to them for reasoned answers.

The rise of digital technology has created a huge amount of often-untapped data sources. These data sources should be utilized to help inform the decisions that are being made in organizations across the world every day. Sadly, due to a lack of education, the resource that could assist in making the right decision the first time is being disregarded in favor of that tried-and-trusted resource, experience.

We are not saying there is no place for experience in decision-making in organizations. You might notice we don't use the term *data-driven* decision-making, as that alludes to how data can be understood to be the sole driving force in making the right decisions. Rather, the best decisions will be made when experience, expertise, and data are combined to create the most holistic view of a situation possible.

We have set this book out in sections that will facilitate your learning about the key aspects of data, and the types of projects developed to implement its use in organizations, so that you can create a culture of *data-informed* decision-making.

Why We Wrote This Book

There is a wealth of books available to teach you about specific data tools and technologies and the different skills you will need to learn if you are to become a data specialist. Carl alone has written one of each so far! Yet we weren't aware of any books that have taken a high-level approach to introducing you both to the skills required to work with data and to how those skills are used when delivering data projects and developing new data products and propositions.

We didn't want this book to become an encyclopedia of "all things data," as you are unlikely to have the time or inclination to consume such knowledge. This book aims instead to be an easily accessible guide that teaches you just enough to build your confidence without bogging you down in details you are unlikely to use regularly, especially if you are leading the projects rather than working hands-on to develop the outputs.

We'll not only walk you through the stages of an example project but reflect on how one individual project is unlikely to create an organization that instinctively makes data-informed decisions. This is why we detail how to develop successful projects into broader data platforms that allow further projects to coherently take the next steps necessary for creating the desired data-informed culture that is seen in the most successful organizations.

The final reason why we have written this book is to broach the subject of data as it should be perceived through the lens of a decision maker who won't have all the skills, or time, to take up each part of the work as an individual. An organization is made up of many people with differing specialties and areas of expertise, so we look at how to create a data-fluent and informed culture without compromising people's valuable contributions to your organization.

Who This Book Is For

If you have picked up this book, it is likely that the title resonated with how you feel about data. You may be curious as to what data really is and what potential it has to help you and your organization. Yes, you probably hear the word at work and home multiple times a day, but very few people can define what it is and even fewer feel comfortable using it purposefully. This book has been written to help you understand data, learn about its key features, and discover what is possible with data, and then covers how to deliver the technical and human parts of a data project. Ultimately, we aim for you to feel empowered with data such that you can drive your organization to become more data informed.

So, who do we assume you are? While this book should assist many people across the organization in different teams and hierarchical levels, we have focused on those leading an organization, or large functions in an organization. We did this for the very reason that those individuals are often time-poor and under pressure to understand complex subjects quickly.

We understand the complexity that comes with data. We have been hands-on with data for decades between us, working in global, complex organizations. We have been responsible for designing, developing, and delivering projects that involve data. This is not an easy task. The task is made harder when leaders haven't had a solid education in all aspects of working with data yet are asked to make detailed decisions on projects involving it. By reading this book, we hope that you will come to understand the challenges and learn from our experience and missteps along the way.

How This Book Is Organized

This book is divided into five chapters. It can be read cover-to-cover to provide a full overview of how to channel your data curiosity into tangible deliverables and the drive towards forming a data-informed culture in your organization. Alternatively, you might want to consume the chapters individually, leaving time between to implement the key insights from each. In particular, the third, fourth, and fifth chapters might be revisited or read on separate occasions, as it's unlikely that you will be able to use the book's guidance while you deliver a single project with a full data platform and team to support it.

Chapter 1 gives the context the rest of the book is based upon. It is very unlikely that everything you read in this chapter will be new to you. The chapter aims to get all readers to the same level of understanding as to why data curiosity is not just a nice-to-have attitude but is essential in a successful modern-day organization and career. The chapter culminates in setting the scene to encourage the creation of a data-informed culture, explaining how it increases the likelihood that an organization is successful.

Chapter 2 fills in the gaps left by the aforementioned deficits in the education system. After defining what data is, the chapter covers data as a resource, the products formed from those resources, and the skills required across the organization to successfully develop data-informed products and propositions.

Chapter 3 walks you through the end-to-end lifecycle of working with data, from acquisition or extraction, through storage, curation, and exploration, to sharing the outputs of the work with others.

Chapter 4 dives deeper into the technological decisions that not only can shape a single project but will empower your organization in the future. The chapter also details how to get started with the technology so it doesn't feel like you are having to make every major decision before testing what is effective for your organization.

Chapter 5 looks at the people involved, where you might find them, and how you might deploy them to make the most significant impact. This chapter also covers who you will need to influence and work with to move towards our desired aim of creating a strong culture of making data-informed decisions.

O'Reilly Online Learning

 For more than 40 years, *O'Reilly Media* has provided technology and business training, knowledge, and insight to help companies succeed.

Our unique network of experts and innovators share their knowledge and expertise through books, articles, and our online learning platform. O'Reilly's online learning platform gives you on-demand access to live training courses, in-depth learning paths, interactive coding environments, and a vast collection of text and video from O'Reilly and 200+ other publishers. For more information, visit *https://oreilly.com*.

How to Contact Us

Please address comments and questions concerning this book to the publisher:

> O'Reilly Media, Inc.
>
> 1005 Gravenstein Highway North
>
> Sebastopol, CA 95472
>
> 800-889-8969 (in the United States or Canada)
>
> 707-829-7019 (international or local)
>
> 707-829-0104 (fax)
>
> *support@oreilly.com*
>
> *https://www.oreilly.com/about/contact.html*

We have a web page for this book, where we list errata, examples, and any additional information. You can access this page at *https://oreil.ly/data-curious-1e*.

For news and information about our books and courses, visit *https://oreilly.com*.

Find us on LinkedIn: *https://linkedin.com/company/oreilly-media*

Follow us on Twitter: *https://twitter.com/oreillymedia*

Watch us on YouTube: *https://youtube.com/oreillymedia*

Acknowledgments

We'd both like to acknowledge the O'Reilly team, who brought the opportunity to write this book to us and helped create a book we are both proud of. Michelle Smith once again trusted Carl to kick off another book to allow him to further explore this subject. The content has been shaped by our development editor, Gary O'Brien, who has diligently pulled our thoughts into a more coherent and approachable form.

We'd also like to thank Chris Love, whose technical reviews helped further certain ideas and provided a critical challenge to some of the concepts we have covered.

CARL ALLCHIN

I would like to make a personal acknowledgment to the man who set an example of a work ethic that enables me to take on these opportunities. Ernie Allchin, my grandfather, passed away as this project came to fruition. Ernie had an unbreakable work ethic that set a tone for me to aspire to. Ernie never had the opportunity to receive a good education nor understood data, but he did support me in my career and life, even when it took him away for extended periods of time. My family is very engineering-centric, so their work was always measured by what you could touch, and writing books has allowed me to create a physical output of my work. Seeing Ernie holding a copy of my books is a proud moment that will not be forgotten.

I would also like to thank my partner, Toni, who encourages me and puts up with me taking on book-writing projects in equal measure. I took a break from writing when my son was born in August 2021, but was lured out of that hiatus by this project. Without Toni's support and Oscar's cuddles, you wouldn't be holding this book now.

One final thanks goes to Sarah, who has taken on two essential roles in this book. Originally, Sarah was a technical reviewer for this book, but due to an extended period of illness, Sarah became a coauthor and primarily wrote the final two chapters of the book. Her technical reviews of the first three chapters enhanced the project dramatically, but her words forming the final two chapters have made the book as strong as it is. Thank you.

SARAH NABELSI

I would like to thank my mom, Maissa, for all her love, support, and endless care for me. Thanks for always believing in me, for always challenging me to be a better version of myself, and for valuing education and hard work. Your role model growing up has made me who I am today and helped my work ethic translate into the authoring of this book.

I would also like to thank my sister, Tasneem; outside of my mom's influence, her impact on my life has been beyond compare. Thank you for all your mentorship, support, and encouragement.

Lastly, I would like to thank my partner, Amit, who jumps at any opportunity to support me on projects like this. Thank you for supporting me through moments of high stress and foregoing time spent together while I pursue this and other projects.

Finally, although I am saddened by the incidents that brought us here, I am thankful to have had the opportunity to coauthor a book with you, Carl. Writing a book is no easy task, and I am so thankful that my first foray into authorship was with you. I'm glad I could be of help to bring this book to life, and my best wishes to you in your recovery!

The Emerging Data Challenge and Opportunity

In 2006, Clive Humby declared, "Data is the new oil,"[1] and the power of that quote caught the attention of many business leaders worldwide. Humby was a co-founder of the leading data analytics firm dunnhumby, who in 1994 delivered a revolutionary customer loyalty scheme for a leading British supermarket, Tesco.[2] The traditional retailer flourished due to the use of data analytics through customers receiving personalized coupons to spend in stores. dunnhumby had shown the power of data, so when Humby spoke those immortal words, you'd have been wise to listen, and the same is still true today.

The pressure for you to create value from your data didn't just come from Humby. Conference talks, business publication covers, or management literature may have brought other trends to your attention. *Big data*, the *Internet of Things* (IoT), *machine learning* (ML), and *artificial intelligence* (AI) are all terms that might keep you up at night. The development of terminology about data solutions seems to be increasing at a pace that is matched only by the speed of the technological development powering it.

If you have reached for this book because you feel behind the curve, you match the majority of stakeholders we talk to every day. Everyone seems to fear that their competitors are ahead of them in terms of collecting and utilizing their data. If you are already utilizing data, you may fear your competitors are using data in a more advanced way that could lure your data gurus away. After all, every tech geek wants to work on the latest challenges using the most advanced technology.

---

1 Michael Kershner, "Data Isn't the New Oil—Time Is," *Forbes Magazine Council Post* (July 15, 2021), *https://oreil.ly/JiJai*.

2 "About Us," dunnhumby, *https://oreil.ly/bL8YU*.

There are many valid reasons why you may be feeling the pressure to up your organization's data capabilities, but we will let you in on a secret...don't believe everything you hear. Not every competitor has gained full control of their data and empowered each individual in their organization to use this capability. Some might be further ahead in their ability to *refine* their data resource, but their journey is likely far from complete.

A study by Accenture showed how far organizations have to go in their quest to make the most of their data.[3] Just 21% of the global workforce is confident in their data literacy skills. Research by Forrester found that between 60 and 73% of enterprise data has never been analyzed.[4] This is not likely to be the same picture you had in your head when reaching for this book, as you are seeing data being increasingly used, but that doesn't mean there aren't further opportunities to harness data. This book will show why data is an asset that you can use to support each decision in your organization and how validating your decisions with data will prevent choosing directions based on incorrect assumptions. The value of being right more of the time is enormous.

This book will introduce you to the key terminology, concepts, and challenges you will encounter when developing a data culture in your organization. To lead the variety of changes required, you need to be able to ask the right questions of many individuals. This chapter will introduce you to the challenges of working with data, why those challenges exist, and how to navigate data projects successfully.

Rapidly Evolving Challenges

Managing change is a given in a modern organization. You are unlikely to have reached your position without being able to deliver projects in a dynamic environment. Developing your organization's data capabilities will also require change management, of both people and processes. Since Humby proclaimed the value of data in 2006, the speed of technical development in data processing, analysis, and regulation has meant change isn't delivered just once but is a flood of constantly evolving capabilities.

When working with data, you will be asked to consider a number of different parts of the end-to-end processes involving data. You will need to think about how to best source, store, clean, analyze, and communicate data. Once you have your solutions in place for any of these challenges within your organization's process, you will quickly find faster and more user-friendly solutions from the new products that continually emerge in the market. As an example, databases used to be the best technology and conceptual approach to hold your organization's data, until the volume of data flowing

---

3 "The Human Impact of Data Literacy," Accenture, 2020, *https://oreil.ly/R7qnk*.

4 "Closing the Data-Value Gap: How to Become Data-Driven and Pivot to the New," Accenture, 2019, *https://oreil.ly/VdmN1*.

into organizations each day grew to the point where people found it necessary to create data lakes. If you had invested in a database, suddenly you were under pressure to adopt a data lake to address changing needs. Recently, *data lakehouses* have emerged as an option to handle the next evolution of challenges posed by working with data in modern organizations. We'll discuss the growth-of-data challenge in more detail in the next section.

Data has become an asset that can create revenue and opportunities to develop your company. As with any possibility for improvement, there are a number of challenges to solve to gain the benefits on offer. Opportunities arising from data are no different in this respect. Products and propositions powered by data can be created from data to allow organizations to develop new revenue streams or deeper relationships with their customers. A *data product* uses data to form the basis of an application or item that wouldn't be possible without its use. A *data proposition* doesn't create a tangible product, but allows for a new or enhanced service.

Let's go into more detail about the challenges you are likely to face when pursuing the opportunities created by data. You will need to keep in mind that even once developed, the products and services themselves present their own set of challenges regarding keeping up-to-date and maintaining the ability to meet the needs of users.

THE GROWTH IN DATA VOLUME AND VELOCITY

The last few decades have seen dramatic changes for those working with data, and it would be foolish to expect any slowdown in this level of change, especially in technology. Trying to keep up with the overall market is virtually impossible, and this is one reason why most data specialists focus on just a handful of tools. The data specialists responsible for working through the end-to-end lifecycle of data in an organization will likely have one tool to support the extraction of data from its source, one tool for storage, and one tool for analysis of the stored data. The need for these advancements is like any technological development; as soon as a solution is created, that solution is used to develop the field you're operating in even further. Most technical developments create new challenges to solve as yesterday's solutions become today's problems, and each new tool rarely delivers a comprehensive result, meaning that ongoing development is required.

Big data is a term that is commonly used when referring to many of the challenges posed by working with data in the 21st century. The definition of big data is not easy to tie down, and it's unlikely that most people agree on it. Three common concepts cited in most definitions stem from Gartner analyst Doug Laney's "3 Vs" in his definition of big data:[5]

---

5 Svetlana Sicular, "Gartner's Big Data Definition Consists of Three Parts, Not to Be Confused with Three 'V''s," *The Gartner Blog Network*, November 11, 2013, *https://oreil.ly/If8EA*.

- Volume: amount of data

- Velocity: speed of data creation/transfer

- Variety: different data available

In 2013, another Gartner analyst, Svetlana Sicular, highlighted that the 3 Vs wasn't the only part of Laney's definition of big data. Sicular cites the importance of the phrase following the 3 Vs that describes the technical solutions required to deal with the challenges. The entire sentence she cites reads, "'Big data' is high-volume, -velocity and -variety information assets that demand cost-effective, innovative forms of information processing for enhanced insight and decision making."[6]

Other challenges can be characterized by:[7]

- Veracity: level of trust in the data

- Variability: uses and formats of the data

- Value: business value of the data

For the common terms, each of these characteristics has increased dramatically over the last two decades with the growth of propositions leveraging the internet and digital connectivity. The volume of data produced globally has grown from 2 zettabytes in 2010 to 26 zettabytes in 2017, and is estimated to have grown to 120 zettabytes by 2023.[8] Your organization will not access all of this data, or even close to it, but the growth pattern is indicative of the volume increase in your own organization. Software that is used to process or analyze data is often referred to as *tools*. Whilst data tools have existed for decades, they have all had to develop the ability to process larger data sets or become redundant. *Data tools* refers to the software used to form, analyze, and communicate data. Their technical development has enabled organizations to do a lot more with data than ever before.

There is never as much time to work with the data as you might want. As data sets have grown, the time available in the working day has stayed the same. Being able to handle the greater velocity needed to absorb, process, and analyze the data has required improved technology and infrastructure. Whereas a bank would once simply collect data on each transaction I made as a customer, my bank now captures data each time I

---

6 Sicular, "Gartner's Big Data Definition Consists of Three Parts."

7 Bridget Botelho and Stephen J. Bigelow, "Definition: Big Data," *TechTarget: Data Management*, January 2022, *https://oreil.ly/7rPOf*.

8 Petroc Taylor, "Volume of Data/Information Created, Captured, Copied, and Consumed Worldwide from 2010 to 2020, with Forecasts from 2021 to 2025," Statista, September 2022, *https://oreil.ly/NZ3js*.

log in to their website or mobile application, capturing the time of the login and what services I used during that interaction. Increasing the number of data points captured about each transaction and interaction means there is more data to process than before, but still within the same amount of time. The data tools we work with require greater speed in collecting and storing this data.

As you will learn in the next chapter, data comes in many formats, and the growth of volume and velocity results in an increasing variety of data forms. Being flexible in what data sets work with your software has become a key requirement.

We'll continue to reference the 3 V challenges posed by big data, as they've become a constant part of the environment all organizations work in. These challenges require rapid technological development to facilitate and respond to the evolving environment. Data specialists have had to acquire new skills and learn new techniques to maintain their specialties.

Data science has become a popular term that encompasses many of these new specialties, such as machine learning and artificial intelligence. In the 2010s, just managing and understanding the data assets built up by organizations was the focus of most data specialists' work. Over the last few years, as this understanding of data assets has developed, specialists have emerged to project forward the information and insights discovered. The development of new tools and technologies has allowed specialists to perform and optimize these predictive and optimization tasks.

NEW REGULATIONS AND GOVERNMENT MANDATES

Change hasn't been driven only by technological developments. As data has become an increasing part of more people's roles and decision-making processes, regulation has increased to protect individuals from potential negative consequences of data analysis.

Working with data now requires understanding the concept of *Personally Identifiable Information* (PII). Government identification codes, postal and email addresses, and phone numbers are just a few examples of data points that organizations must handle very carefully. Just having access to PII isn't the issue—the data that is held alongside it is the important factor. Political affiliation, sexuality, or health information are all sensitive data points that should be tied to individuals only when absolutely necessary.

Regulations like the General Data Protection Regulation (GDPR) in Europe have clarified definitions of PII. Since its introduction in 2016, GDPR has caused many organizations to alter how they hold their customers' and users' data. GDPR has seven principles[9] that set a strong standard for how you should store any data within a data project:

---

9 "A Guide to the Data Protection Principles," Information Commissioner's Office, May 2023, *https://oreil.ly/wDvYV*.

Lawfulness, fairness, and transparency
> The data adheres to all legislation, does not cause an undue detrimental harm to the subject of the data, and they understand why it has been collected.

Purpose limitation
> Data is only collected for a specific purpose and that is clear to the subject of the data.

Data minimization
> The minimal amount of detail is kept to meet the purpose of the data collection.

Accuracy
> The data collected must remain accurate and be deleted once it no longer is.

Storage limitation
> A finite time should be set as to how long the data should be held for.

Integrity and confidentiality
> Security measures should be in place to protect the data held.

Accountability
> You must have clear processes in place to demonstrate your compliance.

The intent of these principles is to ensure that data held about any individual is only for a set purpose, is held for a set time, and remains accurate. An example of why these rules are important is the Cambridge Analytica scandal that came to the public's awareness in 2018. The scandal centered on how a data analysis company used data acquired from Facebook to create links between people and their political preferences. Eighty-seven million people, who just happened to be friends of 270,000 users of a third-party application on Facebook, had their data collected for this purpose, even though they had never agreed to this analysis or use of their data.[10]

Regulations like GDPR also focus on how securely the data is held in the integrity and confidentiality principle. Data breaches and hacks are common news items and can cause issues for millions of people at a time. Passwords and other personal details are frequent, valuable targets for hackers looking to impersonate others or commit crimes like fraud. The security of your data sources is critical. As the volume of data collected has grown with global services like music streaming, activity tracking applications, and the continued use of email, the value of such data security services increases.

---

10 Kurt Wagner, "Here's How Facebook Allowed Cambridge Analytica to Get Data for 50 Million Users," *Vox*, March 17, 2018, *https://oreil.ly/3pYwe*.

In many industries, regulation about data is still forming and evolving and will be a constant source of changes that you will need to balance when developing data solutions.

IMPROVING DECISION-MAKING BY DEMOCRATIZING DATA

For decades, organizations have based their decisions on the experience and expertise of their employees. With the fast pace of technological innovation and increasing scale and scope of most roles in organizations, it's becoming increasingly difficult to just rely on your experience to make the right decisions. Data is not just being requested by your organization's team in the form of financial accounts, but by everyone covering all aspects of the organization, covering customers, operations, and employees.

Banks used to use branch managers to decide who qualified for a loan and who didn't. The bank manager used their own local knowledge, relationship with the individual, and knowledge of the individual's financial attitudes to decide whether they were a safe person to loan money to. This model clearly has a lot of bias, so it was far from ideal to being with, but other issues were also present. What happened when the branch manager left their role? What if a customer was new to the area? The evaluation of loan applications provides one example of the ways in which data available has significantly impacted organizational practices and outcomes.

Companies like Experian use data to form credit ratings that allow financial service providers to assess a person's creditworthiness. A quick look at someone's credit score is often enough to approve or deny a loan request. This is great if you have a strong credit score and a stable financial history, but this isn't the case for everyone. New financial providers have appeared that are focused on those individuals who don't have a good enough credit score and will look at other factors instead to determine if a loan can still be offered. That's right—these providers developed a data solution for a problem that was caused by another data solution, using wider sources of information.

Every organization isn't evaluating loan applications, but each person in your organization is likely making decisions every day that affect your customers, partners, and bottom line. If you have experienced staff, they are likely to make decisions based on their long tenure, and that can work out fine. However, many decisions are made based on new and developing situations or by someone who is still gaining experience. This is where data can add a more rounded perspective on a situation. If you are a senior manager in your organization, you are likely to have the data you need because you know who to ask, and that they will get it for you. However, many junior members and even middle managers in the organizations that I work with struggle to get the information they need to make data-informed decisions.

Democratizing data means getting the right data into the hands of everyone in your organization. This is a key focus of this book and has been a focus throughout our careers. By building data products and propositions that can be used by different groups at different levels of your organization, you will be empowering them to make better decisions.

When analyzing data, it is important to truly understand the core concern being addressed by the analysis. The best people to understand the nature of the key question to be answered are the subject matter experts in the business. Even this is not an easy task to compile, as each individual will likely have different questions they are trying to answer. This means a lot of different data sets, held at different levels of aggregation (a concept we'll come back to in Chapter 2), and different tools may be needed to answer each question. It might seem daunting to provide clarity, focus, and direction amidst all the data and competing priorities, but this book will help you understand how to approach this task and how to be successful in democratizing data.

DEVELOPING NEW PRODUCTS AND PROPOSITIONS

Increasingly, data sets aren't just used for informing decision-making but have become products in their own right. New products and propositions have become possible as the value of the information in the data sets has been found and refined.

Take Beeline, for example. Beeline is a cycling navigation product that simplifies navigation on bikes in urban areas, pointing you towards your destination rather than specifying each left and right turn you need to take. Beeline's initial product was a physical device that fit to your bike's handlebars, with a small screen to act as a compass directing you to your end destination and any waypoints that you specify in the application before you set off. The linked phone application stores your speed, route, and many other data points. This provides the user with a comprehensive view of their trip.

Beeline has monetized this same data by aggregating it across all users and anonymizing it to provide additional data to a diverse set of organizations. Transport planners, local councils, and even retailers can use the data to understand when and where people cycle and how smooth a journey they have. This can inform where investment in dedicated cycling infrastructure is needed, or where to locate new stores to serve those who are cycling to the area. I (Carl) know I appreciate the choice of cafes at the end of my cycling commute to refuel before I start my working day.

As discussed earlier in "New Regulations and Government Mandates" on page 5, GDPR forces the possessor of the data to ensure it is held only when there is a clear purpose specified to the end user. This makes forming data products and propositions from the data harder, as they almost need to be scoped out before the data set gets collected. But as long as the subjects of the data are clear on what you are doing with it, data propositions do become possible to create. Maybe Humby was right after all when he said that data is as valuable as oil? Just like oil, the data needs to be refined (read, cleaned, and prepared), but many data sets have multiple ways in which they can be valuable to different organizations.

BUILDING A COMMON UNDERSTANDING

With so many possible approaches for so many people in your organization, it can be difficult to get the right data, at the right time, and in the right way for them all. In many organizations, data is provided by central teams who maintain data sources. With the increasing demand for data to inform decisions, these teams are often stretched thin, with limited time to understand how to best meet your requirements.

Depending on the size of the organization, the central data teams can be very removed in terms of subject matter knowledge and physical location from the requestor. To collect the requirements and then deliver upon them, most central teams have traditionally worked in the form of waterfall-style projects, especially for larger requests involving creating data sources. Waterfall-style projects involve *stage gates,* a term that refers to the process of signing off on progress in stages as the project develops. Whilst the waterfall model once had its benefits for many IT projects, it has become less relevant to data projects that require significant iteration. Waterfall projects need the questions to be answered by the data set to be established at the start of a project. However, when working with data, as soon as you find an insight, you will discover that different questions arise that then need to be answered. It is difficult to predict what these questions might pertain to, and it's therefore often not possible to include them in those initial requirements. This means that waterfall-style projects often deliver outcomes that quickly become redundant as requirements develop. This can lead to new projects being raised, or stakeholders may stop using data to guide their decisions.

Traditionally, special teams were also set up to provide reports and insights to the subject matter experts (SMEs) in the business to save the data experts in IT teams for more architectural projects. This organizational structure was created because data tools were complex to learn to use and required a skill set that many people didn't have; thus, all business users couldn't be trained to utilize the tools.

What the requestor needs is the ability to ask and answer questions rapidly and iterate quickly themselves. For example, if you are looking at the causes of customer service complaints in your organization, you would want a report counting the root causes for each complaint. You might want a report that breaks these numbers down by product, over time and by location. But as soon as you find the causes of the complaints, you will probably have many more questions that are hard to predict without the answer to the initial question. As you gain more experience working with data and as your organization's data teams work more closely with business SMEs, you will begin to ask better questions.

In my experience, few of the people requesting data insights are comfortable asking for what they really want, for a number of reasons:

- They don't want to look stupid if what they are asking for doesn't exist.

- They haven't seen what the art of the possible is with the data tools, so they don't know what can be done with data.

- They may ask for only a small part of their overall needs because they assume it takes too much effort to achieve the whole request.

- They may not have the resources available to complete the full request, so they ask only for part of their needs.

Challenging Data Issues

As soon as you can navigate the challenges that come with working with data in modern organizations, a larger one looms—people. As with most changes you look to make in your organization, shifting people's attitudes and behaviors is likely to be the hardest part. Change related to data has an additional barrier, as there is a common perception that anything involving data is difficult, technical, and specialized.

I've spent the majority of the last decade battling this perception of data. There is no one single reason why data is seen this way, but the lack of presence of data in primary school and college education is a big factor. Filling the knowledge gaps left by academia over the previous few decades is one of the largest challenges currently faced by organizations.

Imagine that your team is unable to read and understand the words used in emails and other written messages. How much impact would this have? Emails wouldn't be understood, reports would be left unread, and learning would be impeded by the inability to pick up a book to learn from. Why would we expect data to be any different? This demonstrates the importance of being able to understand and communicate with data.

Simply working with data isn't enough in the modern organization. Cultivating a culture that supports challenging common conceptions and norms regarding data is important to making any progress towards empowering people with data. From the executive to the front line, having an expectation that data be present in decision-making is just as important as using any other experience when establishing courses of action. Ensuring there are positive attitudes towards using data when making decisions is vital in creating a strong, progressive culture, as what has always been used in the past—in other words, experience—needs to be tested against empirical evidence.

Even where data is pervasive in decision-making, care should be taken as to how fragmented the data ecosystem is within your organization. The *data ecosystem* is how all of the data sources, analysis, and products work together. Not all sources of data are easy to use across different tools. Data specialists often prefer certain tools, and this can create some tribalism within your organization, preventing the collaboration you desire.

DATA FLUENCY

Being fluent means you have the ability to express yourself with ease. Data fluency refers to the ability to express yourself with data. In a modern organization, what does this look like?

Reading data involves many different skills, depending on how refined the data is. If the data has come directly from the source that created it, reading it often involves processing it before using a tool to look at the data more closely. *Processing data* involves cleaning, merging, and restructuring it to prepare it for analysis. If the data comes from a more refined source, it's likely to be easier to read and to have a clear structure or a graphical output. The second chapter of this book will cover the types of data files and how you might work with them.

Creating graphical outputs from data sources has been written about widely (including by Carl Allchin in *Communicating with Data*, published by O'Reilly) but is a critical skill for everyone in the modern world. To be able to create effective charts and graphs, you first need to be able to read data and understand what makes a chart effective and what doesn't. The understanding of data visualization and communication effectiveness is an emerging field, but general best practices are already known. Data fluency is often referred to as understanding these best practices and principles.

Just understanding how to read graphical outputs of data sets is not enough; you need to be able to communicate your findings. This communication is often achieved through creating your own charts and graphs to highlight the insights you've uncovered, as visual understanding and pattern recognition are highly efficient interpretive skills for humans.

We've used the word *understanding* a lot in this section of the book and, for us, this is the key part of data literacy. Reading and writing are important, but it is the understanding you take from the data that is most important.

Being able to critically analyze the data outputs used in your organization is vital to getting the value out of the data assets within it. Just as with written literature, going beyond the words on the page is important to see the true meaning, and you will benefit from being skeptical about what data products are shared with you.

Data visualization is a powerful communication tool, but it is difficult to produce without bias. This isn't to say you shouldn't trust the data outputs in your organization, but you should try to understand their source, figure out the intent behind their production, and identify anything that could have been left out.[11]

Should you ignore data because of its potential flaws? In a book called *Data Curious*, you probably can guess the answer to this question—no! W. Edwards Deming's

---

11 Ben Jones, in *How to Avoid Data Pitfalls* (O'Reilly, 2019), and Alberto Cairo, in *How Charts Lie* (O'Reilly, 2019), have written excellent books on avoiding these issues when building data visualizations.

quote, "Without data you're just another person with an opinion,"[12] is one that I (Carl) personally love. In all organizations, it's difficult to separate personal opinions and politics when making decisions. Having evidence to back up your opinions is vital when challenging the status quo and truly trying to find weaknesses in your organization.

Therefore, creating a data-fluent workforce is important to ensure everyone is able to read, question the information that is shared with them, and express their own points with data.

DATA CULTURE

Creating a data-fluent workforce is not enough to gain the benefits of data. You need to create an organizational culture that looks to actively use data in its decision-making processes. If your organization doesn't have the inclination to support business cases and new proposition ideas with data, it can be quite a challenge to promote this.

Data cultures are often formed when new leaders come into organizations. These leaders frequently come from organizations where strong data cultures are present, and they expect the same capabilities to be present in their new teams. If you are used to having information to support business cases, it can feel lacking not to have them.

Data-informed decision-making is where data is used to support or challenge business cases and propositions. Informed is the key word, as decisions aren't led by data, but additional evidence is offered to help make the right decision.

Using data to support decision-making can be pushed further, to where data-driven decision-making occurs. This is where empirical data evidence takes precedence over non-data arguments like someone's experience. There is a fear frequently found in organizations with weaker data cultures that if the data points to a certain decision, it can't be overruled. This fear can prevent people from being open to using data at all if they feel like their ideas or experience will be ignored completely. This concept should be dismissed as quickly as possible to prevent resistance to using any data at all.

The creation of a data culture must be fostered by at least a mid-level manager but often needs leadership sponsorship. This is due to the cost involved, of software solutions, additional hires, or the expert support you might have to leverage to help establish data solutions or form the strategy required.

An organization's leadership can provide crucial momentum towards more data-informed decisions by asking for data to support the decisions they are being asked to make. This is ultimately the main factor in creating a strong data culture. Organizations are designed to respond to the requests of the leadership, so if they request data products, then they are likely to get them. Middle managers can show the value of

---

12 Milo Jones and Philippe Silberzahn, "Without an Opinion, You're Just Another Person with Data," *Forbes*, March 15, 2016, *https://oreil.ly/bTKXG*.

using data to help guide their decisions to their leaders. This doesn't mean it will be easy to form what they ask for, especially if their teams aren't data literate.

The more requests for data that are made, the more the organization will see data as part of the decision-making process. Practice might not always make perfect, but it is definitely a step in the right direction.

CONFLICTING PREFERENCES

As data becomes more frequently used across your organization, you may start to experience other challenges. There are many data tools to choose from when preparing, storing, or analyzing the data. To create a strong data culture that involves sharing and collaborating data sets to help improve your organization's decisions, you need to limit the number of similar data tools used. This is for a number of reasons:

User interfaces
Unsurprisingly, each piece of software will have different user controls and processes. A different screen layout can reduce efficiency when working. Any barrier to a user getting what they need as quickly as they expect will likely stop the tool from becoming the go-to option it might be otherwise. When using different interfaces, training has to be offered, which incurs cost.

Technical differences
Not every data tool in the same category, i.e., acquisition, storing, or analysis, is functionally identical. Tools have differences, from the calculations you can produce to what data can be easily connected to. This can lead to duplications of data sources, as each tool may need its own version.

Knowledge sharing
This is a key aspect of working with data but can get lost when different tools create different factions of data workers. Knowledge sharing about how to optimize the use of the tool is very useful, but not sharing the insights found is a concern of even greater significance.

Purchasing
By using multiple tools in your organization, you are less likely to be able to generate economies of scale. Most software purchases are made on the basis that the larger the purchase is in volume, the lower the value per license or credit will be.

None of these issues is an absolute showstopper. Having different tools can help; different tools can make hiring easier, as you have a wider pool of talent to recruit from. However, if you've put the time and effort in to raise data literacy levels and build a data culture, you will want to harness as much benefit as possible, so focusing on a few key pieces of software will help considerably.

What Does Data Empowerment Look Like?

Managing change and the process of improving your organization's data skills can seem to be a long, challenging journey, but it is worth the effort. Microstrategy has reported that organizations using data analytics have "faster, more effective decision making."[13] The same report also noted the following benefits:

- Improved efficiency and productivity (64%)

- Better financial performance (51%)

- Identification and creation of new product and service revenue (46%)

- Improved customer acquisition and retention (46%)

- Improved customer experiences (44%)

All of these attributes are clearly attractive to any organization. *Data empowerment* is not just about making faster, more effective decisions; it's about giving people the data access to form the information they need to make those decisions, find revenue opportunities, and improve customer retention. Access to data sets alone will not enable your people to be empowered with data, but giving them access to easy-to-use tools and the knowledge of how to work with data can. Ensuring people see the role that data has in decision-making at all levels will encourage them to challenge the status quo when analysis and insights point to the benefit of doing so.

Let's get into more detail about what data empowerment looks like for your people and the processes they will work on.

PEOPLE

The 2020 Microstrategy report also shares that respondents said that 76% of executives have easy access to data, but only 52% of frontline employees do. Clearly, it's important to support strategic decisions with data. However, if everyone isn't able to do so, missteps are still likely being made, or opportunities are not being taken. Coupled with inadequate data literacy skills for their roles, there are a lot of potential improvements to be made.

In *Communicating with Data*, I (Carl) wrote about the growing importance of being able to influence change through the use of data, in the same way that words and numbers have been used to form arguments supporting decisions in organizations since their inception. Data, in the form of charts, graphs, and summary numbers, have become increasingly important parts of forming influential arguments. Therefore, it's

---

13 "2020 Global State of Enterprise Analytics," *MicroStrategy, https://oreil.ly/rmwQY.*

important for all levels of the organization to be able to access data and have the skills to analyze it, or some may become unable to influence as strongly as others.

Data access goes beyond just accessing the data sets created from the systems they are originally captured in and involves having the skills and tools to form analyses. If tools are intuitive and easy to access, your teams at all levels of the organization will be able to use data to supplement their knowledge and expertise. Being data-empowered means not only that issues can be found but that ideas can be supported by using data as evidence for why something should be done. Communicating with data should make the articulation of ideas far clearer and empirically supported, removing politics and influencing skills from decision-making at more levels of the organization.

If your team feels they can challenge processes, validate decisions, and innovate, they will be more engaged with the organization, rather than feeling frustrated or ignored.

PROCESSES

Organizations have used business analysts, somewhat effectively, to find and solve problems for a long time. Empowering all your team with data could create an army of business analysts rather than having to bring in people with those skills.

With increased access to data and skills, data can be utilized to move fluidly through changes required by your organization, find causes of known problems, and propose solutions that wouldn't have been possible otherwise. Common techniques like Six Sigma and many other forms of process improvement rely on putting data in the hands of the people who understand the processes where issues or inefficiencies exist. The data points are used to identify where customers are asked to take unnecessary steps or where clients have to take the same steps repeatedly due to poor organizational processes. Being able to access the relevant data allows people to measure the impacts of the inefficiencies they find in their work or hear about from customers in their interactions.

When I (Carl) worked for Barclays Bank, we saw a dramatic improvement in reducing the number of complaints and resolving the issues they caused by making data more accessible to key decision-makers and leaders.[14] We used interactive dashboards to allow everyone from the executive team to the frontline operational teams to access daily trends in what issues had arisen and caused complaints. Before these were in place, it took weeks to turn round the analysis that pinpointed where in the organization the complaints were originating from so they could be addressed. This meant that the issues creating complaints continued to happen before finally being addressed weeks later, after even more complaints had arisen.

---

14 "Putting the Data in the Hands of Stakeholders Using Parameters at Barclays," *Tableau*, June 2, 2014, *https://oreil.ly/ONx7p*.

For any improvements that are made, measuring the impact is just as important as the change itself, to ensure that they are as effective as intended. Although executives make the decision to implement a solution, the actual implementation is conducted by frontline teams. When frontline staff are allowed to see the impacts that changes have, they are more likely to support them or suggest improvements if the changes are not having the desired effect.

DATA-INFORMED DECISION-MAKING

One fear about using data to make decisions has to do with where to draw the line between relying on human experience and thoughts versus just looking for answers from the data available. We use the term *data-informed decision-making* to highlight the role we believe data should play when making decisions in organizations. Fear can center on data pointing in one direction and being forced to follow that direction unquestionably. This is commonly called *data-driven decision-making*. Following anything unquestionably is never a good thing, as common conventions will never be a perfect fit forever.

With data solutions becoming more intelligent, there is a temptation to lean in the direction of data-driven decision-making, but the full context and situation are rarely captured by the data available. There is a lot of growth in data science, machine learning, and artificial intelligence, but before these solutions can be fully leveraged, the data sources need to be collated and validated. Most organizations are currently struggling to gather all the data necessary and then check that the data sets used to make decisions are correct.

Even with comprehensive data sources, human thinking is still ahead of computer-based decision-making in many cases. The gap is reducing rapidly, but having human skepticism by questioning the models used to make data-based decisions is still important. Data can be an additional factor in making decisions but shouldn't be the only one. This merging of data with other factors is what we refer to as *data-informed decision-making*.

With the clear benefits of informing decisions with data for both people and processes established, your next question is, How do I get started? Depending on the state of your data sources and levels of analysis, there are many routes available to creating a culture of data-informed decision-making.

The rest of this book will look at the following key questions:

- What is data, where is it created, and what can you make with it?

- How do you acquire, store, curate, and share data products?

- How do you build analytical products?

- How do you set up a team to deliver this?

Data Knowledge and Skills

Data is the foundation of this entire book. By reading it, you are clearly taking an important step towards using data more than you are today, so it's vital that you truly understand what we mean by data. One of the biggest challenges you may encounter when working with data is the terminology used to describe the values, fields, and files you will use.

Once you are familiar with the terminology, this chapter will introduce you to the fundamental concepts of data. These building blocks of data take many forms. By understanding where data comes from, you will be able to find useful sources, spot differences between them, and learn about what it takes to form a usable data source.

Finding and refining a data source for analysis to drive data-informed decisions isn't the only output you are likely to create when working with data. This chapter will look at the various outputs your projects might create and at the key aspects of each type, as well as describing the essential factors that ensure each meets the project's requirements.

As covered in Chapter 1, data fluency is a fundamental set of skills that are likely missing for many people in your organization. To create the benefit of data-informed decision-making and build valuable data propositions, you will need to fill this skill gap for yourself and others. The abilities required to ensure successful project outcomes will be covered so you know what aptitudes and expertise are required to achieve the best results for your organization.

What Is Data?

Data is the facts or numbers collected from observations for the purpose of understanding a particular subject better. This can include the details or figures that operational systems create to record transactions for future reference within the system or for reporting purposes. Compared to the trickle of data produced when, for example, books were handwritten or census data was collected manually, the amount of data produced by increasing digitalization and the greater adoption of smart devices has become a flood.

The challenge of working with data is no longer just about finding the right data sets amongst the sea of data available but now lies in "wrangling" the data available to find answers to your questions. Using new data sources can often involve cleaning, structuring, and aggregating data sets into more easily usable formats. These tasks involve planning what is required, investigating the data, and then enacting those plans to form a revised data set for further analysis. Finding these sources of data will involve a lot of collaboration with colleagues as you track down the data that will help you achieve your goals.

To understand what data is needed, you will need to be able to translate the business problem at hand into a question and form hypotheses to test. There is rarely a single way to resolve a dilemma, and you will need to iterate through various formulations to learn what solution is really required. Gaining experience of refining the questions to get to the true need requires experience, and developing trust with your stakeholders will require time and effort.

Organizations have built valuable data stores over the past few decades; or rather, their IT departments have, as they were the only people with the experience required to do this type of work. These stores were, until recently, hidden behind layers of security and required specialized knowledge to access them. During the last decade, software solutions addressing these barriers have changed not just who can work with data but how quickly they can access it.

Organizations frequently need to restructure, clean up values, convert codes to actual names, and join multiple sources together to make data usable. Specialists often conduct this work, but even when that is the case, the better you understand the tasks involved and the parts of a data set, the more likely you will be to get the data you need at your first request. Also, software has become more usable for ordinary users by becoming no, or low, code platforms. This means you don't need to learn specialist coding languages to begin to access data sources yourself. The following section will help you learn how to form your own data sets from the sources in your organization.

KEY FEATURES OF DATA

There are many different features of a data set. Many of the terms will be familiar to you, but some may be new concepts; we'll cover them in this section.

Some features determine the shape and structure of the data. These include:

- Columns

- Rows
- Headers

Other features of data sets change how the data can be used. These include:

- Categories
- Measures
- Data types
- Granularity

When you ask most people what comes to mind when they think of data, you will be likely to hear the word *spreadsheet*. Spreadsheets are very useful, flexible data stores and places where data can be analyzed through tables or by creating charts. In many ways, spreadsheets contain many of the common features of more scalable and specialized data solutions.

Most data sources provided by IT in your organization will be classed as *structured*. You can usually see the structure of the rows and columns within a spreadsheet due to the gridlines shown. This means the data sources have the following components:

- Columns: a single column should contain a single attribute of the data and can be only one type of data.
- Rows: each row should contain a single recording of an instance in the data.
- Headers: a title for a column details what is within it.

A *record* is an individual transaction or instance captured in the data. As rows contain records, these terms can be used interchangeably when discussing data sets.

Not all of your data sets will be held in this clean format. *Clean data* refers to data that is well-structured and can easily be analyzed in its current state. *Unclean* data is the opposite of this. Features of unclean data include the following issues:

- Columns: multiple items of data can be included in each individual column, like the third row of data in the Detail column in Table 2-1, which contains the instructor, calories burned, and music listened to during the spin class.
- Rows: a single record can be spread across multiple rows, meaning that values might be missing in each row, or the rows may be repeated; this is often referred to as *duplicate records*.
- Headers: headers might be incomprehensible or not present at all.

Table 2-1. Basic spreadsheet of spin data

Date	Value	Units	Type	Detail
08/01/2023	88.2	km	Tour	Lille to Bruges
10/01/2023	6.1	km	Casual	To the market
10/01/2023	30	min	Spin	Kym - 540 - everything rock
11/01/2023	18.4	km	Commute	Wed 11th morning commute
11/01/2023	18.7	km	Commute	Wed 11th afternoon commute
14/01/2023	20	min	Spin	Sherica - 323 - latest hits
15/01/2023	6.8	km	Casual	Sun 15th shopping

A single column, also known as a *data field*, will likely fall into one of two types, categorical or measure. Before we look in more detail at each in turn, we'll show you how to identify them within the questions you may be asked to base your analysis on. If you are asked a question like "What was the revenue by quarter?" which part of the question is the category, and which is the measure? The numeric part of the question is the measure; in this case, it's revenue. The categorical data is indicated by the additional parts of the question that help specify how the measure is to be analyzed: in this case, by quarter. The "by" part of a question is the bit that will help you identify the categories, starting from the measures.

A *category* is a data field that describes an aspect of what the record is about. When you combine the categorical data fields, you should be able to determine exactly what that record represents. In Table 2-1, each of Carl's cycling activities is described by the categorical data fields of Date (when the activity happened), Units (how the activity was measured), Type (what was the activity), and Detail (extra information about the activity). Categorical data fields often have a limited number of variables that they can contain. The data set from Table 2-1, which records Carl's cycling activities, has only a few possible values in the categorical field of *Type*, like whether the ride occurred on a cycling tour, spin class, or commute. If you hear the term *dimension*, this is another word to describe a category in your data set.

Being able to look at a data set to understand how ready it is to be analyzed is a key part of any data project. Data sets may take many minutes, hours, or even days to restructure to meet the characteristics detailed in this section, before they can become easily usable. In Table 2-1, the Detail column contains a variety of different types of descriptions of Carl's cycle rides. This means that anyone who wants to count how many times he listened to a certain type of music in a spin class will find it more difficult to do so than if there was a separate "music type" column.

Measures are often the numerical values in a data set that lie at the heart of what you are trying to analyze. Measures are rarely looked at on an individual row-by-row basis but are often instead aggregated across many rows of data. Take these typical questions that you might be asked: What was the sales total for February? What was the average daily attendance for the last quarter? The sales values are summed up by month, whereas attendance is presented as an average across a quarter. You are likely to perform these aggregations when analyzing the data in your analytics software.

Not all numerical data points are treated as measures. You will often find that data sets have *identifier* fields that can be used to differentiate records from each other. Maybe you have a data set of all your customers where, rather than holding all their details, like name and address, you use a numerical identifier to differentiate customers. Numerical values are often used as identifier fields, as they require less memory to be stored or used in queries on the data set. Identifiers can also be used to obscure the data to make it harder to identify who the data is about. Because the identifier is used to differentiate records, the data field is classified as a category rather than a measure. Totaling up these identifier fields rarely yields anything useful.

What each row of data represents is the final key feature of data sets you'll need to understand. The term *granularity* is used to describe at what level of detail each row exists. As categorical data fields describe the different elements that rows reference, they are key to understanding the granularity. Let's use Table 2-1 to show how to define the granularity of a data set.

In Table 2-1, Date, Units, Type, and Detail can all be used as categorical data fields, but which are setting the granularity? A field having the same value as another row is a sign that it can't set the granularity of the data alone, unless the row is a duplicate of another row. Date, Units, and Type all contain the same value in multiple rows, so don't set the granularity inherently. Detail is a description of each ride Carl takes, so even if he has undertaken the same activity, the Detail field is very likely to be unique from any other value found in the same column.

The data set in Table 2-1 doesn't have to be held at the granularity of each ride on a specific day. You could summarize the data set to describe how many rides happened each day (Table 2-2). The morning and afternoon commute rides on 11th January 2023 have been combined to describe the number of activities undertaken on that day for the same type of activity. The records for the 10th January 2023 can't be combined, as they represent different types of rides that are also measured differently. Conversion from minutes to kilometers ridden, or vice versa, will have to be made if the Value data field is to remain in the table.

Table 2-2. Summarized data set from Table 2-1

Date	Value	Units	Type	Number of rides
08/01/2023	88.2	km	Tour	1
10/01/2023	6.1	km	Casual	1
10/01/2023	30	min	Spin	1
11/01/2023	37.1	km	Commute	2

Date	Value	Units	Type	Number of rides
14/01/2023	20	min	Spin	1
15/01/2023	6.8	min	Casual	1

When using a data set, if you see a field that is likely to be an aggregation, then you might want to assume there has been some *pre-processing* of the data set. In Table 2-2, the number of rides is likely to be an aggregation, as each other row represents a single record detailing a single activity, whereas the fourth row captures the details of two rides at once. Like any source of information, to understand any potential biases or errors that could have been introduced by the changes, you should question the source of the information and who made the changes.

DATA TYPES

In the definition of a column of data, we highlighted that each column should have only one type of data, or data type. A *data type* is the classification given to a data field that establishes what we can do to it. Let's describe each main data type and what you can do with them.

Numbers

We all know that numbers come in two formats: whole and decimal numbers. Numeric data values will be made up of 1s, 2s, 3s, 4s, 5s, 6s, 7s, 8s, 9s, or 0s. Numbers will frequently be aggregated when conducting an analysis of a data set.

When whole numbers are used in data, we commonly refer to them as *integers*. Decimal numbers are commonly known as floating point numbers, or *floats* for short. These data fields are more likely to be those that you aggregate or search within for individual values to answer your specific questions.

Aggregating numerical data involves summing, averaging, or counting values. Numerical data fields can be aggregated in many different ways depending on the questions you have been presented with. This happens when you are trying to answer questions such as the following:

- What is the total sales value?

- What is the average grade achieved?

- What is the maximum attendance of any of the events?

Aggregation often involves splitting the data up by categories found in the data set before aggregating. This happens when you are asking questions such as the following:

- What is the total sales value for each month?

- What is the average grade achieved for each subject?
- What is the maximum attendance for any event for each genre of music?

Notice how the numeric data is still at the heart of each of these questions, but remember that you also need to understand the categorical data fields.

String data

String data fields contain alphanumeric values along with punctuation and other symbols. Many computer programs will default to treating a data field as a string if it isn't specified in the file's formatting because they are the most flexible as to what characters they can contain. String data fields will make up the majority of the categorical fields in your data set. Understanding what your string fields represent will help you understand what your data set contains and what it doesn't.

Values in string data fields are treated differently from numeric fields. You can still aggregate string fields in a few ways, such as the following:

- Counting the number of times each value is found
- Finding the minimum or maximum value based on alphabetic order
- Listing all the contents in a single value

String fields can be split apart or appended to other string fields by using a variety of calculation functions to ensure they are useful for the questions you are trying to answer. Taking the detail field in Table 2-1, you'd need to split apart the three different attributes that are currently squished together into one field. Strings can be split based on a specific character, on a pattern of characters, or by the position of a character. In Table 2-1, the variables in the Detail data field could be split apart based on the hyphen. You could use calculations to create new data fields that would record the trainer of the spin class, the calories burned by Carl, and the music the session was performed to, respectively.

Position is a useful concept to understand when using string data, as it differs from numeric, date, and Boolean data fields. *Position* refers to the order of the characters found in string field values (Figure 2-1). Each character, whether a letter, number, or symbol, has a position you can reference in calculations.

Figure 2-1. How position is determined in a string field

As string fields can contain a vast array of characters, they take up more storage space in databases and take more computing power to process than numeric fields. Database administrators (DBAs) will look to ensure data is stored and processed as efficiently as possible.

Date fields

Date fields are also an inefficient way to store data. Some software will allow you to store dates in a common format, such as that shown in Figure 2-2.

Figure 2-2. Date field format

While this format is easy for people to read, from a computer point of view, there is a significant storage and processing overhead. For this reason, you might find date data held in many different formats specific to the software you are using. A couple of examples of these are listed here:

Excel serial number

If you have ever had a date suddenly change to a number in Excel when you change the formatting, this is probably why. Excel stores dates as an integer per day from January 1st, 1900. Using 12/31/2023 as an example, the Excel serial number equivalent is 45289.

Epoch date

Epoch date works similarly to an Excel serial number but uses an integer per second from January 1st, 1970, at midnight. Again, using the date in Figure 2-2 as an example, the epoch date value would be 1703890800.

As mentioned in "Numbers" on page 22, integers are efficient ways to store values, which is why they are used instead of in a human-friendly format. You will need to convert the values to a readable format if you are planning to share the data set with humans.

Boolean fields

To make your database administrator happy, try to store as much data in a Boolean format as possible. Computers fundamentally use 1s and 0s to operate, and a Boolean data format is just 1s and 0s. The 1s and 0s represent true or false, or yes or no, as to whether a record has a given characteristic or not. This means computers can store and retrieve Boolean values much more easily than other data formats.

In large organizations, you will frequently encounter database extracts, or data sets taken from databases, that use 1s and 0s as indicators for yes and no within the data set. For example, when holding data about what banking products a customer had, 1 and 0 indicators would simply store which of the products available each customer had. This allows for quick formation of summaries across millions of rows of data (Table 2-3).

Table 2-3. Boolean data used as indicators for yes/no

Customer ID	Cash account ind	Savings account ind	Credit card ind	Trading account ind
7005461	0	1	0	1
9174324	1	1	1	1
5094878	1	1	1	0
4168373	0	1	0	0
1511246	1	0	0	0
2380267	1	0	0	0
6792839	1	0	0	0
5022090	0	1	0	1

As with dates, you may want to apply an alias to the indicators to make the data clear as to whether the 1 or 0 means yes or no. This will help others who might use the data source to understand what the 1s and 0s represent.

DATA FILE STRUCTURES AND FORMATS

The data types and terminology used to describe the parts of a data set are just the beginning. You will also need to understand the terms used to define where and how data sets are stored. Your computer is likely filled with the most common formats of data sources, Excel spreadsheets, but you may not have directly used the largest data storage format by volume in the world: databases.

Files of data such as spreadsheets are very common due to the flexibility they offer in how they hold data. This same flexibility of input makes it much harder to use the data found in spreadsheets as a source for further analysis.

The shape of data

There are two main forms of data that you will find in most spreadsheets: columnar data and pivot tables.

You are likely questioning what we mean by the *columnar form* of data. This is where data is still held within structured columns, similar to what you would find if you queried the database where the data is stored. Tables 2-3 and 2-4 are simple examples of columnar data sets.

Table 2-4. Columnar data: target sales for stores

Quarter	Store	Target
I	Manchester	475
I	London	475
I	Leeds	490
I	York	490
I	Birmingham	475
2	Manchester	300
2	London	325
2	Leeds	325
2	York	300
2	Birmingham	325
3	Manchester	300
3	London	300
3	Leeds	300
3	York	300
3	Birmingham	300
4	Manchester	330
4	London	400
4	Leeds	400
4	York	330
4	Birmingham	400

It's unlikely that you are first coming across the concepts of pivot tables in this book, but we want to ensure that we are thinking about how and why they are used so frequently. *Pivot tables*, or crosstabs, as they are also known, are quick forms of summarizing large data sets into more easily consumable data points or so that they can be easily used to answer analytical questions. Take, for example, the data table on bike sale targets for different stores found in Table 2-4.

Converting this data to a pivot table allows you to easily reference quarterly trends within the target areas. As pivot tables can contain totals and alternate aggregations, you can use them to find answers to your questions. In Figure 2-3, a pivot table has been formed from the data found in Table 2-4 to organize the data by store and quarter, as well as to create an average target per store for each quarter, and an average across the entire year for each store, in the Grand Total column. The final cell of the pivot table, found in the Grand Total column and Grand Total row, expresses the average target for all the stores across the entire year.

AVERAGE of Target	Quarter				
Store	1	2	3	4	Grand Total
Birmingham	475	325	300	400	375
Leeds	490	325	300	400	378.75
London	475	325	300	400	375
Manchester	475	300	300	330	351.25
York	490	300	300	330	355
Grand Total	481	315	300	372	367

Figure 2-3. Pivot table created in Google Sheets from the data in Table 2-4

For many people, analyzing data in spreadsheets is all the data analysis techniques they were taught in school or the earlier parts of their careers. This has resulted in lots of data being held in spreadsheets either in the columnar form or as a pivot table.

The shape of data is important, as it will suggest what considerations you need to take when working with each form. As pivot tables will likely have had some sort of aggregation applied to them, it can be difficult to determine the source of the data that they are formed from. Many pivot tables are shared across an organization, making the origin challenging to track. Without detailed notes, documentation, or filenaming conventions, it can be precarious to use the tables as the basis of your decision-making. There are several pieces of information that may be missing:

- The origin of the data
- The age of the data
- Any filters or calculations that have been applied

This isn't to say that extracts from databases still in the columnar form are perfect data sources to use. Databases are notorious for having more computer-friendly data field names rather than something meaningful to the user of the data set. Preparation of data sets for analysis often involves clarifying exactly what each contains through better naming and documentation. The origin, age, and filtering may also be issues if the extract of the data source has been shared across the organization. *Data governance* is the term used to describe the tasks undertaken to ensure the data is well documented so its origin, age, and any changes can be tracked and understood by all who need to use it.

File types

There are many file types that will hold useful data sources for you. While you will have likely been using spreadsheets and CSV files throughout your career, spatial files may be new to you, but when used can provide a new dimension to your understanding of your organization. Other file types, like PDFs, may contain useful data sets, but extracting the data from them into the tool where you are conducting your analysis isn't always consistent or straightforward. There are too many file types where data resides to handle in this book, so we'll focus on the most common or useful. When using each, there are a number of considerations you should take into account:

Spreadsheets

The most common data file types within your organization are spreadsheets—usually Excel, Google Sheets, or an equivalent. These files can contain manually input data, pivot tables, or database extracts, to name but a few sources. Spreadsheets were probably the first place where you tried to prepare data and started conducting some analysis on that data.

Spreadsheets are a resource you can't ignore when working with data. Due to the flexible input and easy editing of data, spreadsheets are common locations where your peers will model forecasts or apply their knowledge of a subject to derive meaning from the data.

However, the ability to enter data values, apply calculations, or remove data points means you should take care whenever using any spreadsheet as a data source. It's very easy to make mistakes such as mistyping a value or wrongly directing a calculation towards the wrong data values in a spreadsheet's cells.

Most business intelligence (BI) tools need to have data held in clear columns with a single header. When shared across an organization, spreadsheets are often formatted to have more detailed titles and other commentary inserted above or alongside the data tables you might want to use when analyzing data. This means spreadsheets have to be reformatted by removing the additional titles and text before they can be analyzed with BI tools.

Comma-separated value (CSV) files

You can open CSV files within many of the same types of software you use for spreadsheets. The main difference is the structure of how the data is saved. Each row of a CSV file should contain a single record, but each of the data fields are separated by a comma instead of having columns of data. As an example, the first row of data in Table 2-4 would be held as 1,Manchester,475.

Spatial

If you work with data that details things like the position, distance between, or area covered by stores or people, it is likely that you already use spatial files that hold information about how to map data points when conducting geospatial analyses. Spatial files may not be common in your industry, but if you encounter them, there are some key differences that you will need to consider. Spatial files contain data about points (specific locations), lines (routes), or polygons (areas on maps). These files don't come as a single file, but as a directory or folder of files. For example, the Esri shape format contains .shp, .shx, and .dbf files. You will likely need special geospatial software or business intelligence tools to open spatial formats, although more business intelligence tools are making this type of analysis easier to conduct alongside more traditional charting.

Going beyond files

Not all data sets will be in files on your computer or network. Most data in your organization is likely held in a database. Databases are structured stores of data held on computers. Most databases are large enough to require specialized computers, known as *servers*, with specifications suited for storing and processing high volumes of data.

Database providers, such as Microsoft, Oracle, Teradata, and Snowflake, to name but a few, compete over the speed to absorb, process, and deliver data sets to users. How the databases handle these tasks has developed over time, and much of this processing happens within the database without the user of the database ever seeing it. In the most common form of databases, relational databases, the layers of a database that the user does see are the tables and views.

Relational databases store similar data in tables that can be related to each other through shared identifiers or other data fields. For example, a client might have their contact details held in one table and the billings they've accrued in another. For the two tables to be used to send the billings due to the client, you'd need to join the tables together on a common field found in both tables. The tables in a database hold rows and columns in the same way as other data sources we have shown.

For example, a customer of a bank will probably be part of many data queries:

- What products does the customer have?

- What's the customer's credit limit?

- What branches has the customer visited?

- What channels does the customer use to transact with the bank?

- Does the customer have any shared products with other bank customers?

If all this data were stored in a single table, it would be monstrous and unruly. This is why the data is broken down into different tables—to make it more manageable. The bank will likely store the data in separate tables. The table names are illustrative of what they might be called in the organization's database, like in the following example:

Product_Customers
> Contains which products a customer has and the services they use, when they started using the bank, and whether there are any other customers listed on the account.

Detailed_Product
> Each product has different interest rates; also indicated is the date on which the product was sold, and to whom.

Branch_Customers
> Details which branch locations a customer has visited.

Digital_Interactions
> Contains a list of interactions a customer has had with the bank, when they occurred, and through what channel; examples include depositing a check in a branch, taking out cash through an ATM, and transferring a balance through the bank's mobile application.

This is just part of the overall jigsaw puzzle of data each company has about consumers, clients, or customers. Databases don't come with an off-the-shelf solution that will match your organization's data sets or needs. You'll need a specialist to design a structure for the database. This specialist is often called a *data architect,* and their responsibilities include architecting data products to meet the analytical, operational, and strategic needs of the organization. The data architect will help decide what sets of tables are needed to gain information from the data, how they can be linked together, and how data will be loaded, read, and deleted from those tables.

The fields in each table that act as the links between the tables are known as *keys.* Each row within the tables should have a data field that is a *unique key* linking a record to other data tables to form a complete data set. The unique key, or *primary key* (PK) as they are also known, is treated carefully to ensure each row can be linked to the relevant information in other tables without creating duplication of records. For example, a Customer table should have only a single record for each customer. Therefore, if each customer has their own CustomerID value, this will act as the primary key. CustomerID will also be found in other tables, like product, billing, and address details tables, and can be used to link the different tables together to add the additional information required about each customer, depending on the analysis being carried out.

Not every record has a single-row-to-single-row link. For example, a joint bank account will have two customer records that are linked to that account. This is called a *one-to-many relationship.*

The way a relational database maps together is called a *schema*. This is like a map to navigate how tables are joined together. The schema allows you to form the queries you need to get hold of the data to answer the questions posed. An example of a portion of a banking data schema can be seen in Figure 2-4.

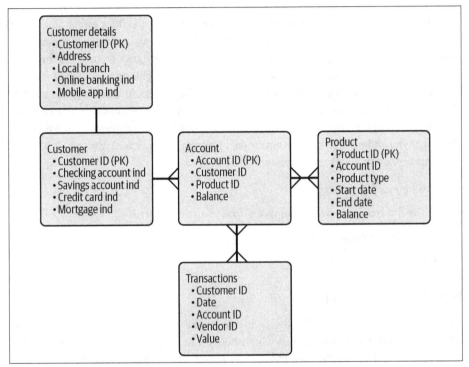

Figure 2-4. Part of a schema

As data can be looked at from many different perspectives, you may need to link a single record with many other pieces of information to answer specific questions. This is where relational databases come into their own, as they allow different users to use similar records in different ways.

When working with data in a database, you might need more than the latest data—you may also need historical data. For example, simply knowing a customer's latest balance is useful, but knowing how their balance has changed over many months and years is a better way to gauge the revenue you could generate from the customer's afflu-ence. If a customer was saving for a large purchase like a house or car, then their cur-rent balance could be very low, but that doesn't mean that holding their cash with your bank hasn't been beneficial or that they don't have the ability to grow their assets again.

Historic snapshots of data can take up a significant amount of storage space, espe-cially if each snapshot consists of millions of records. You will need to manage the retention of the data to ensure that you are only storing data that is of potential value to you and that doesn't surpass the subject's data rights as discussed in "New Regulations and Government Mandates" on page 5.

Data as a Resource

Now that you know what data consists of and how it can be stored for either ad hoc use in files or more strategically in databases, you need to understand where it comes from originally. Understanding the journey your data sets have gone through before they reach you is important for many reasons, including avoiding bias and potential errors.

With more members of your organization gaining access to data, keeping track of the data sources and the changes made to them can become harder if not carefully managed. Managing your data from source to consumption requires an overhead of effort that you will need to plan into your data projects, but it is well worth it.

This section will look at the following key issues:

- Where data is created
- The difference between operational and analytical sources
- How to curate data sources
- Governing data sources

WHERE DATA IS CREATED

Quite frankly...everywhere. The digitalization of the world means that most of your activity, purchases, and interactions with others create data points. Even within my lifetime, capturing data has changed from a very intentional act to a consequence of life.

When I (Carl) was born less than 40 years ago, data was captured through intentional means like surveys or paper forms. When my son was born last year, it felt bizarre when we had to manually enter data into a form or fill out anything on paper rather than the data being automatically generated.

This digitalization has led to the growth of the variety and volume of data available. The opportunity to learn more about your clients, customers, and consumers without having to ask them continually to supply data points manually is huge. With such a range of data sources, let's look at a select few and why they may prove to be fruitful sources:

Online shopping
  Shopping in a physical retail store in the late 1990s provides a great example of what information most stores wanted about their customers but would have to manually collect. Staff would try to upsell customers based on what they were either looking at or holding in their hand. The creation of long-lasting

relationships with customers happened through signing up the customer to their mailing list or catalog.

The digital environment has become much more retailer-friendly. Customer details are obtained through collecting an email address on offers or during the checkout process. Upselling happens based on the cookies that track the journey of the customer through the internet, which alludes to what else they might be interested in. Bespoke links can be easily attached to marketing messages, QR codes, and offers to see what acquisition methods are most effective. If the promotion comes from a social media site, you are likely to be able to determine many of the demographic factors that will help you pitch subsequent enticing products and offers to them. The collection of this data occurs without much extra effort from the customer; therefore, the retailer can collect it easily and accurately.

Smartphone

About a decade ago, another avenue was opened up for collecting customer data: motor insurance. In 2012, my former employer, Aviva, offered drivers the chance to download an app that used the sensors and GPS data available in a smartphone to monitor how safely someone was driving. The better the driving style exemplified by their minimizing of sudden braking and speeding, the more premiums would be reduced from the standard rates.

This product, although revolutionary in the UK at the time, met with a lot of skepticism, as smartphones and the data they were able to collect about their owners were only just beginning to be recognized and monetized. Consumers were cautious as to whether the discount was worth being increasingly monitored, in terms of the locations where they were driving as well as having their driving assessed at all times.

Smart devices/quantified self

Smart devices are products that connect to the internet or leveraged algorithms to offer additional services or enhancements to the original purpose of the product. Although manufacturers tried to create mass market appeal for such devices as far back as the 1980s, it was their pairing with phones that really created a desirable proposition. Subsequently, smartwatches were one of the first types of smart devices that used the growth in smartphones to make a mass market impact.

In 2015, Apple launched the Apple Watch, which originally measured steps and linked to your phone but has slowly developed into a medical tracker of heart rates and activity and even offers monitoring of heart health through electrocardiography. These features have allowed Apple to pair the watch with fitness training to allow you to monitor how hard you are pushing yourself in gym classes taken at home. I used my smartwatch to track my classes at home to see whether I (Carl) was burning more calories per session and what classes were the most effective (Figure 2-5). I have also been able to analyze the impact on my "free time" of the arrival of my first child in the summer of 2021.

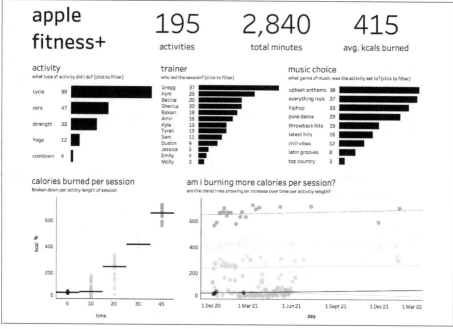

Figure 2-5. Carl's fitness tracking using data from his smartwatch (a larger version of this figure is available at https://oreil.ly/de7fI).

This data can be shared by the owner with other service providers for many purposes, including healthcare provision. In the UK, health insurance provider Vitality has created a novel insurance product that reduces premiums and offers cashback and reductions for retailers if customers meet activity targets.

As the data generated about everything increases, a balance must be struck between scaring customers about how much we know about them and the enhanced propositions we can offer them. Customers who have grown up in the 21st century are already used to surrendering their data to have a more personalized experience. However, there are limits to what people are happy to have monitored, despite becoming increasingly accustomed to their data being used. You can't just assume people will be OK with very nuanced decisions made about them based on their data. Organizing focus groups of customers to test propositions and how they might affect your organization's reputation is wise.

OPERATIONAL VERSUS ANALYTICAL SOURCES

With data being created continuously, data sources have the challenge of absorbing data at the rate at which it is created. This is one of the reasons why the traditional *Extract, Transform, and Load* (ETL) convention has changed to *Extract, Load, and Transform* (ELT). It's difficult to process data at the speed of creation, so it's easier to first absorb all of the data and then transform it into the sources you need for analysis at a later stage.

Data sources that haven't been transformed from their original structure are often referred to as *operational*, whereas those that have are called *analytical* data sources.

Operational data sources are the data sets that are created for the purpose of offering the services, products, or monitoring that your organization does. For example, in an insurance company, the operational systems will capture the client's details in the insurance policies, monthly premiums paid, and any claims made. The data set often comprises the memory of the system, storing all the records that capture the transactions processed by the system. The systems are designed for a process, and therefore, the data sources are often a byproduct of the main purpose of the system. This means they are not structured for the purpose of analysis or use elsewhere. If you want to analyze the data contained within these data sets, you're going to need to augment and reshape the data. This transformation will happen in an analytical database that is separate from the operational data source (Figure 2-6).

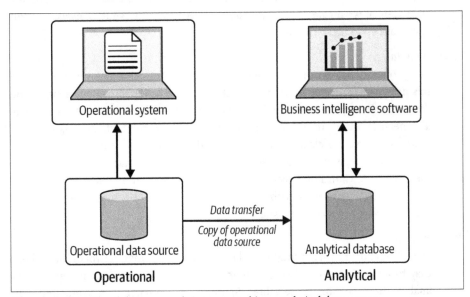

Figure 2-6. Operational data sources being converted into analytical data sources

The data contained within the transactions is what is likely to be analyzed by business intelligence (BI) analysts. Finding outliers and identifying trends in the data set will help to decide your organization's next steps or set out what needs to be improved. Aggregating measures or counting categorical variables will allow the BI analysts to find outliers and trends. Care has to be taken to understand whether the findings are being swayed by any extreme outlying values, especially when using averages. Most BI tools use a default average of a mean. These can be altered dramatically by a few very large or small numbers. Using medians can help reduce this effect. Identifying the outliers can be useful as they are often the transactions that can help identify new opportunities that weren't previously thought possible.

Data sets taken directly from operational systems are rarely ready for analysis. This is where you are likely to need to transform your data from its original structure in the operational system into something better suited for analysis. Whether your organization uses an ETL or an ELT methodology, the T is the transformation step. The transformation involves reshaping, cleaning, and removing unnecessary data points. Exactly what needs to be done for analysis will differ, but some of the common steps will involve the following tasks:

Aggregating data

When you are looking for trends in your data and overall patterns of client behavior, it's unlikely you will need all of the details of each transaction. If you have a clear view of what categorical data points are important to your analysis, you can aggregate up to these factors.

Cleaning data

Many operational systems will have data field names that are unclear for the business expert. By renaming these fields to more understandable versions, the data set will become much easier to use. The data values within the fields may also need cleaning up to make the analysis easier to conduct. Various transformations to create a clean data set, as mentioned in "Key Features of Data" on page 18, will depend in each case on which operational system you are sourcing the data from. Common tasks involve removing rogue numbers or letters in values, filtering out records with null measures, or creating basic calculations to make analysis of measures easier.

Reshaping data

Operational data sources might not be structured in a manner that makes them easy to analyze. Having a single column per value is important if you need to analyze the data using those values. Splitting amalgamated data points into individual data fields will ensure the data fields are available to the analysts.

Reshaping data may also involve pivoting data to ensure each row represents an individual record and each column represents a categorical value or measure.

Combining data sets

Taking data from an operational data source might not tell you everything you need to know to analyze the data. You are likely to need to pair the data set with other data sets to provide context as to why the transactions occur in the way they do. Factors we frequently look to add to operational data sets are product descriptions, marketing campaigns, and customer histories.

Ultimately, what you need to do to prepare data sets for analysis is to think through what questions you need to answer. This will allow you to ensure you are refining the operational data to the best level of aggregation, cleaning the data fields you'll need in your analysis, and adding in any additional fields from other sources to help make sense of your data.

CURATING DATA SOURCES

Once you have determined if you need an operational or analytical data source, your next task is to see if others require the data set too. I have frequently found that if I can use the data set to answer questions I have, others will find the data useful too.

Operational data sets can be prepared for use by ensuring they are in a format suitable for the software they will be used with. This might involve changing where the data is stored or the shape of the data. If you query the operational data, the last thing you want is to have any subsequent effects on the operational processes that use the system. Running queries on an operational system's databases could cause issues if you process vast volumes of data or write a query that changes the data in any way. The best way to avoid any undue impacts is to work on a copy of the data, as shown in Figure 2-6. Although this duplicates the storage of the data for your organization, queries can be run against the data without fear of any impacts.

By making a copy of the data, you also have the opportunity to prepare the data for its use. You may want to remove sensitive data, such as PII, and replace it with identifiers, or split up any different data values that sit together under one field into more easily used data fields.

Analytical data sets are likely to require much greater levels of transformation. Analytical data sets are formed to answer specific questions and address particular areas of investigation. These data sets power lots of the reporting and insights that you will already have access to in your organization. They are likely to comprise a number of data sets that originate a lot of the reporting you receive. These data sources shouldn't change dramatically, as any changes made can have an impact on the reports and dashboards that they power. Changing data field names or restructuring the data set will mean the reports and dashboards will need to be rebuilt to match the edits.

If you are building a running data project that will create a new data source, it's likely you will require many iterations of the scope of the data source. When you design a data source to develop your reporting from, you will inevitably learn from the insights in the reporting that will mean further questions arise. If you stick to the original scope, you will leave your users frustrated that they can't get the answers they want. However, if you let changes continue forever, then you will never deliver the project. Being ready for some iteration when planning a project is important, but setting a time limit for user feedback is a way to limit the impact.

The skill set to build the data source is rarely found within the same team as the SMEs asking the questions about the data. Creating clear communication channels between these individuals will be key to both sides being able to interpret the needs of the other. I've found having the data set developers sitting with the SMEs can help people quickly communicate the changes needed, but take care to also preface the conversations with why the question is being asked, in case the developers can add additional suggestions. This avoids the situation where each side gets frustrated with the other for changing the requirements too much or taking too long in situations involving technical challenges to meet the requirements.

With the rise of remote working after the COVID-19 lockdowns, sitting in close proximity to each other has become much harder. This isn't to say that this point should be ignored, however. Creating clear virtual and digital communication channels for each side to work closely together, whether physically or digitally, will help ensure the iteration process happens quickly and effectively. I've found it really valuable to have regular sessions between SMEs and the technology teams building the data sources, not just to discuss progress on individual projects but also to facilitate a general sharing of thoughts on what is needed in the data set or processes governing the data sets.

THE BLESSING AND CURSE OF DATA SOURCES

If you have been able to create data sources to help you inform more of your organization's decisions with data, you will now face an additional challenge: maintaining those sources. Data governance will be delved into in more depth in the next chapter on a more macro level, but for now, just remember that ensuring your project has good data controls in place is important. *Data governance* involves how data should be gathered, stored, used, and disposed of.

Project resources are often established to run a developmental project but then are further utilized for other tasks. Creating a data source is a positive step, but it will require continued management, monitoring, and maintenance to ensure the data remains consistent and complete. The long-term ownership of a data source is one area that is often neglected but can make the difference between something that is useful in just the short term and good for the long term.

When you have established your data source, you will need to consider the following tasks to ensure it stays fit for use:

Checking that refreshes have processed

Your data source may just be a snapshot in time of a data set, but it's likely that it will continue to update with the latest data. Especially if the data source is valuable, with rich insights, you will want to ensure you are still basing your decisions on the latest information. Data sources refresh on many different schedules: hourly, daily, weekly, and monthly, to name but a few. Ensuring the refresh of the data set has run correctly is a worthwhile task. Errors can occur based on issues with the source, changing data structures, errors within the transformation steps, or errors loading the refreshed data set into where it is stored.

Changing content

In the first chapter, we covered how, as people learn, they will ask new questions of a data set. The data source will need to be updated with the new fields or changing levels of aggregation to meet the new needs.

Changes in the use of the data source

A data source is often set up for the software it is to be used with. As new software emerges in your organization, you will need to meet its requirements in order for the data source to remain relevant.

Changes in legislation

Data sources should be set up with expiry dates when they will no longer be relevant, but they also need to be managed in case new legislation requires changes. Ensuring there are people responsible for this means the data sets will be governed to meet all requirements.

No longer required

Removing a data source when it is no longer required is a frequently forgotten step. Due to the disconnect between business domain experts and technical teams, it's often overlooked that the change in the original purpose for the data source needs to be shared. This means the management overhead costs for that source continue even when there is no benefit being derived from it. Validating data sources is a useful task to undertake in order to reduce unnecessary effort in maintaining an ever-growing list of data sources.

Managing data sources might seem like a potentially costly overhead, but actually it's a great sign for an organization. Having data sources people want to use and continue to develop means the benefit is still being derived from the initial investment in them, so the task shouldn't be neglected.

Data Products

The development of data sources and the data products that are formed from them go hand in hand. In the early years of data analysis, the majority of effort was focused on using data to answer questions about the organization. The value of data has more recently been focused not just on making better decisions but on creating revenue-generating products and propositions from data sets. There is a range of products and propositions that can be developed from data to fit your and your clients' varying needs.

The term *data product* is used to describe the resulting work created from the data. The product is unlikely to be a tangible object that you can feel or hold. The results of working with data can be anything—a table, chart, report, or dashboard, to name but a few. We will also use the term *proposition* when the data is used to create a service that relies on data but isn't just focused on sharing a data product. This section will go through the various types of products and how they are developed.

TYPES OF ANALYTICAL OUTPUT

Data can be processed for many different reasons; this section will go through the most common types of output that you will come across in most organizations. The following sections have been ordered in terms of the sophistication in the use of data it takes to form them.

Operational reporting

Operational reporting is often produced to answer simple, repeatable questions that need to be answered regularly. Operational teams are frequently asked to undertake repeatable tasks. The time it takes to complete a task, the accuracy of the work, and the volume of the tasks are all valuable data points that help plan the number of people required to complete the work.

Operational reporting is likely to include snapshots of activity through counts of tasks completed, trends in activity, and amount of work remaining to be completed. Reporting is used internally to optimize performance or externally to measure contractual compliance for any work that is outsourced by your clients.

Many teams in your organization will want to receive operational reports to help them understand how efficiently work is being completed; this will help managers inform their decision-making. The industry you work in will determine what you want to achieve through operational reporting. Let's look at a few industries to see how they use operational reporting:

Manufacturing
By measuring how many products you are making, the level of errors discovered and any operational downtime will determine how many products you have for sale.

Call center

The most expensive variable cost for services that operate call centers is having to add extra agents to answer calls. Get this right and you'll be able to handle the demand if there is a surge of calls. Get it wrong and you'll have complaints from your customers and potentially lost sales. Tracking the number of calls, the time it takes to deal with each, and ensuring there are always enough agents available to take the calls will mean your service is deemed to be at least adequate.

Retail

Having the ability to track stock in warehouses, between locations, and in stores can mean that your products are in the right place at the right time. Being able to share these snapshots can let the salespeople in your stores inform your customers in a knowledgeable manner.

Operational reporting is not designed to find the reasons something occurs or spot outliers but to check what level of activity happened on a particular date or range of dates.

The challenge of operational reporting is making sure the reports are produced frequently, often daily, and are filtered to the right team/store/manufacturing line. The term *burst reporting* represents how these reports are created quickly and distributed across an organization.

Supplementing other communications

Charts and graphs are often produced to supplement other reports and communications. They are most frequently made using snippets of data sets in spreadsheets to create charts for presentation slides or emails. Spreadsheets are ubiquitous enough that most people can build basic charts from cleanly organized data sets.

The first data team I (Carl) managed was responsible for creating insights by using extracts from the organization's database in Excel. The tables, charts, and graphs were sent to the teams who requested them but were often then further shared through slide decks and emails in multi-team discussions about performance.

The challenge with the charts in slide decks and emails is that they are frequently sent to other teams and individuals in the organization beyond the original requestor. It's great when your data products are useful to not just the first audience you have built it for, but others as well. However, I've found that when people pass on the outputs of my work, they often do as partial screenshots of the work that don't have any data source details nor link to the creator nor any mention of the filters or conditions applied. This has a twofold impact as, firstly, the screenshot could easily be taken out of context and, secondly, no one will know who to go to for a refreshed view when the data underlying the charts is updated.

This is also a challenge with spreadsheet outputs—they are not inherently designed for repeatability. Spreadsheets are flexible tools to create bespoke work, but this flexibility means that repeating the same process over and over isn't easy. Data is often manipulated within the spreadsheet before the same tool is used to create the charts. This is a challenging process to document and repeat, especially if the outputs are shared around the organization, and potentially to third parties as well. Specialist data tools are required if the work is found useful and needs to be repeated. If spreadsheets remain a core part of the toolkit of working with data, then documentation within the spreadsheets needs to become part of their production and amendment.

Basic data visualizations/analysis

The first use of specialist tools, often using BI software, is usually to create basic reports to answer very specific questions. These tools can create more advanced data products because they are designed to explore and report data to others. Using more advanced functionality of BI tools will require training for the users.

BI tools are increasingly being marketed to business users rather than specialist IT teams. While these tools are becoming easier to use through interface amendments such as dragging and dropping icons around the screen rather than coding, foundational knowledge of how to shape the data sources for use with these tools is still required.

One advantage of BI tools over spreadsheets is the volume and variety of data they can handle. BI tools are designed to connect to data files as well as databases. This access to databases means there is an easier transition to the practice of refreshing the data set for the latest view of a subject.

As these assets get used repeatedly, they are likely to be productionalized. *Productionalized* refers to the process taken to document progress, establish data pipelines, and schedule refreshes of the work.

Dashboards

The early definition of a BI dashboard was a way to see all your key metrics on one screen, like a car's dashboard.

The role and purpose of BI dashboards have evolved and now encompass a much broader definition. This breadth hasn't always been welcomed. Stephen Few, a thought leader in visual analytical thinking, revised his original definition in response to the evolving use of the term *dashboard* in the data world, from:

A dashboard is a visual display of the most important information needed to achieve one or more objectives that has been consolidated on a single computer screen so it can be monitored at a glance.

to:

A dashboard is a predominantly visual information display that people use to monitor current conditions that require a timely response to fulfill a specific role.[1]

Few is focused on the importance of rapid decision-making as a key part of a data product being a dashboard. There are broader definitions that Few disputes, such as the one found in the *Big Book of Dashboards*:

A dashboard is a visual display of data used to monitor conditions and/or facilitate understanding.[2]

To understand what most people in your organization would class as a dashboard, you don't need to prescribe to a precise definition. You will need to know what is commonly referred to as a dashboard in your organization to properly understand what someone actually needs.

One of the key elements of a dashboard is the use of multiple charts in a single page. By having multiple charts, the single view can present different perspectives at the same time. This is where a well-constructed dashboard can differ from the other data products presented in this chapter. By having a more rounded view of a situation, you are likely to make better-informed decisions.

Let's look at a dashboard you might come across if you are trying to understand your organization's IT support tickets, which are raised whenever someone has an issue (Figure 2-7).

---

1 Stephen Few, "There's Nothing Mere About Semantics," *Perceptual Edge Blog*, March 19, 2010, *https://oreil.ly/98j7Y*.

2 Steve Wexler, Jeffrey Shaffer, and Andy Cotgreave, *The Big Book of Dashboards: Visualizing Your Data Using Real-World Business Scenarios* (Hoboken, NJ: John Wiley & Sons, 2017).

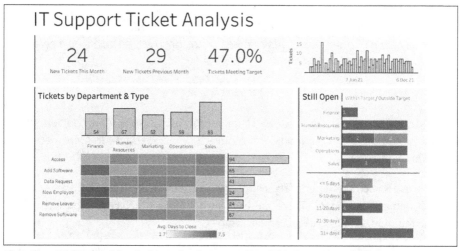

Figure 2-7. IT support ticket dashboard (a larger version of this figure is available at https://oreil.ly/VCOVB)

From this dashboard, you can understand the volume of tickets in several different ways:

- Raised this month
- Raised in the previous month
- Solved within the SLA[3]
- Raised by each department
- By each reason
- Still to be resolved
- By the time outstanding

Just like forming a data source, your dashboard needs to be created with the questions it has to solve kept in mind. The challenge with a dashboard is trying to draw the line between presenting enough information without offering too much. The dashboard in Figure 2-7 shows a lot of information that not only allows for the monitoring of a situation but also should assist with understanding why the situation is what it is.

---

3 We're sure you have come across service-level agreements (SLAs) in your career so far, but just in case you haven't: an SLA is an agreement on the frequency and timeliness of providing a product or service. For example, with data products, SLAs will state when the product will be refreshed with the latest data.

Does it answer every question everyone has in the organization? Probably not. For example, you wouldn't be able to track the progress of an individual ticket.

It is rare for any organization not to have BI dashboards. The need for dashboards to make data-informed decisions at all levels of your organization means there is probably a proliferation of them. Just like data sources, they need to be managed to ensure they are still relevant and are being used to answer pressing questions. There is a danger when dashboards are the only accessible way to access data for many if they don't have the skills or tools to query the data directly themselves. If the dashboards available aren't directly able to answer the questions being asked, there is a danger of drawing incorrect conclusions.

Due to the accessibility of dashboards, they are often an effective entry point for many people to start using data. The level of complexity of the charts used within dashboards is one of the major considerations needed to ensure the data is understandable for all users. Using dashboards to help people understand what is available in the data sources in your organization will help develop more advanced analytics in the long run.

Predictive models

One of the more advanced methods of analyzing data is building predictive models to look not just at what has happened in the past, but to try to determine what will happen in the future. The analogy of trying to drive a car by just using the rearview mirror is a strong message as to why you need to develop predictive models. These models are not easy to create, as there are a few specialist skills required beyond what most analysts in your organization will likely possess.

Firstly, you need to have a strong understanding of your data to ensure you build on solid foundations. Through thorough analysis and regular use of data to inform decisions, data sets become better understood and more robust as SMEs use them. This regular use of a data set allows the data to be paired with what the SMEs expect to see within the data. As predictive models rely on data as an input to work out what will happen in the future, the quality of the input will ensure the output is more likely to be trusted and understood.

Secondly, your team will require statistical skills and knowledge to form the models. The skills required to build these models and the methods used to apply the techniques accurately are complex. The rise in the role of data scientists in organizations has occurred due to their ability to create, assess, and optimize predictive models. If you want to learn more about what is possible with predictive models, there are many books, courses, and videos to guide your inquiry.

Just as you will learn from the outputs of other data products leading to you asking different or evolving questions of the data, the same will happen to the outputs you form from predictive models. As you change processes and alter decisions based on predictive models, you will need to retrain the predictive models to fit the current conditions.

DATA VISUALIZATION BEST PRACTICES

Whether you are creating a single chart, developing a dashboard, or trying to show the outputs from a predictive model, data visualizations will make your analysis easier to consume for most people. Data visualization relies on using pre-attentive attributes to allow humans to spot trends, outliers, and patterns quickly.

Pre-attentive attributes are visual representations of data humans can understand without much conscious effort. There are many pre-attentive attributes you can use when visualizing data, but some are more effective than others. Figure 2-8 shows a number of the attributes you will probably find yourself frequently employing.

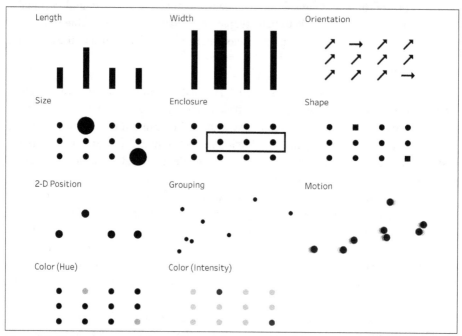

Figure 2-8. Common pre-attentive attributes (a larger version of this figure is available at https://oreil.ly/TGUBk)

Length is the strongest pre-attentive attribute. Bar charts represent the most common use of length when visualizing data. There's a caveat, though. As length is so well perceived by humans, whenever you remove the zero point on an axis, it makes it very difficult to see the true pattern in the data. The zero point on an axis is where an axis starts at 0. If the values shown by the axis don't fluctuate by a lot, it can be difficult to see the variation within the data. We read bar charts by looking at the pattern formed by the length of the bars and the difference between them. Figure 2-9 shows a bar chart. Can you spot the variance in the length of the bar charts? Which stores are performing well? Which stores are struggling badly?

Figure 2-9. A bar chart with no zero line can be misleading

Now, look at Figure 2-10. It's the same data, but this time the axis doesn't start at 2300, but at 0. Would you still answer all those questions in the same way? We built the charts, and *we* would answer them differently! By removing the zero axis, your chart can focus on each of the ends of the bars. It is tempting to highlight the differences between the store sales rather than the total volumes per store. You can do that, but you shouldn't use a bar chart.

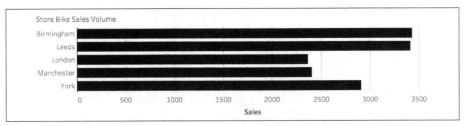

Figure 2-10. Bar chart of store bike sales volume

2-D position is another key pre-attentive attribute that you will frequently use when visualizing data. The 2-D position is used in a number of chart types, but they are most commonly used in scatterplots where the value of each data point is shown based on its position relative to both the vertical and horizontal axes. Scatterplots are a great way to show the correlation between two measures. Each plot on a scatterplot is referenced by its position against the horizontal and vertical axes. The scatterplot in Figure 2-11 doesn't show a strong correlation, but this doesn't mean analytical findings are not possible to discover.

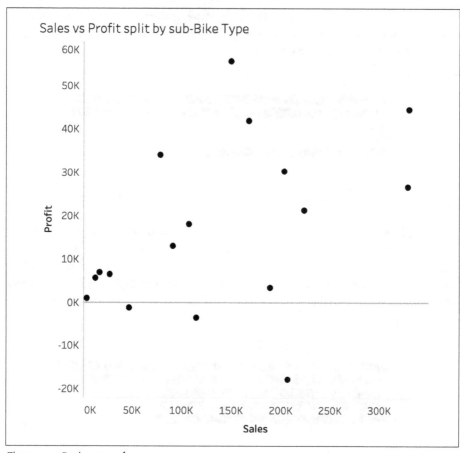

Figure 2-11. Basic scatterplot

By creating average lines off each axis, a quadrant chart is formed (Figure 2-12). Each quadrant can be labeled to help those less familiar with scatterplots interpret the insights within them.

Figure 2-12. Quadrant chart

The final key pre-attentive attribute to initially focus on is the hue of the marks on the page. Hue can be used to help individual data points or sections of an analytical view stand out amongst many others. In Figure 2-13, all 32 boroughs of London have their data visualized, which makes finding one borough to compare to the others challenging. I've used a different hue to stand out from the darker other marks to draw the attention of the viewer.

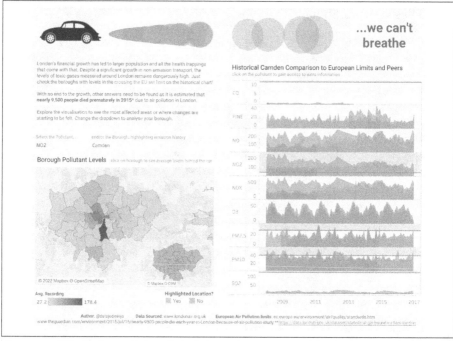

Figure 2-13. "We Can't Breathe" analytical view (a larger version of this figure is available at https://oreil.ly/A4Pza)

Hue is an attribute frequently used not only to draw attention to the marks on the page but also to the work itself. Many companies will leverage brand color schemes in analytical work. Figure 2-14 shows an example of an infographic for a mocked-up airline, Prep Air, measuring its revenue. Prep Air's brand colors are blue and purple, and each has been used to show positive or negative changes.

The challenge with hue is to not overuse it. Coloring every mark on the page with a variety of colors overpowers people's pre-attentive awareness of hue and oversaturates the image, making the trends less legible to the viewer.

Learning how to utilize the different pre-attentive attributes will allow you to find key insights in the data, but they will also allow you to share those same insights with others.

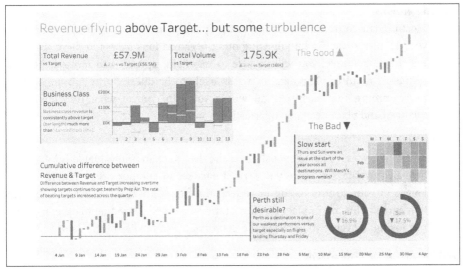

Figure 2-14. Prep Air revenue infographic (a larger version of this figure is available at https://oreil.ly/C4cXY)

DATA SETS AS THE PRODUCT

Another data product is the actual data set itself. Taking Humby's "Data is the new oil" quote further, a refined data set is similar to refined oil, a more useful entity than the input.

As discussed in "Curating Data Sources" on page 37, the process of taking an input data set, structuring it for analysis, and making sense of the contents can be a time-consuming task. Do not underestimate the value injected by adding clarity to the contents and preparing it for other users. When you are preparing the data set for your own or an internal user's use, you might be creating a data set that is useful for others outside of your organization.

Sharing the data sets beyond your own organization must be approached with care. You will need to check that the subjects of the data have granted permission for it to be used beyond your organization, or you risk breaking data protection regulations.

You can share data sets beyond your organization in a number of ways:

Aggregated

The easiest way to adhere to most data protection regulations is to aggregate the results so individual data records are not identifiable. The value for most organizations is to look at more macro trends than just individual behavior, so this reduced granularity does not come at the expense of making the data set redundant to the purchaser. Beeline, the cycling application mentioned in Chapter 1, is a prime example of the value that can be created from aggregated data points.

Hosted solutions

Hosting data sources involves you creating data sources and holding them within your IT infrastructure but allowing other organizations access to them. By hosting the data source, you will be able to maintain, update, and remove the data source as required. The data source is likely to be queried through application programming interfaces (APIs), where you can control what information is accessed and place limits on queries if required.

Snapshots

You might want to issue snapshots of the data to share the valuable information held in the data set. Once you send a data set to another organization, it's no longer in your control to edit or refresh the data. Care must be taken to ensure that agreements are in place to prevent the data being passed on to others, or you risk losing the value you have in the possession and the use of the data.

IMPORTANCE OF ITERATION

Iteration is one of the most important aspects of creating data products. As you work with others using data products, you will learn from the insights you gain together and, in turn, ask new, more varied questions. No matter how good you are at scoping initial requirements for what is needed from the product, you have to keep in mind that those needs will evolve over time.

Preparing the budget, time, and people required to make changes to the product is important and inevitable. Being prepared to iterate will make the process easier and more timely.

The people involved with using a product will make a significant difference as to how complicated changing it will be:

Just you

This is the easiest change process to manage. You will know when changes are made and the likely effects of them. Ensuring the changes are made correctly is important and is the main overhead iterating the data product will have.

Your team

As soon as you start sharing a data product with others, you will need to communicate clearly when iterations will be made and the effects they will have. Depending on the change, you may impact how others are using the product, and this may alter whether they find it valuable or not. Removing data fields or changing the functionality might prevent them from getting what they need.

Your department/organization

As a data product is used by others further away from your everyday role, the importance of communication and version control rises. Stakeholders and users of the data product should be notified of changes ahead of time, tested as to the impact it will have on them, and checked later to ensure they are effective once made.

Others outside your organization

The challenges posed by iterating a data product for your wider organization are potentially multiplied when managing product changes beyond your organizational walls. If the organization has entered into contracts with third parties, you need to consider the changes' effects to ensure the services contracted are still able to be performed.

It may feel that you've now become a product manager, rather than what you initially expected when creating the initial data solution. There are many roles needed to make a successful data product and establish a strong culture of making data-informed decisions. The people aspect of data teams is covered more widely in the fifth chapter of this book. Overall, if many people are gaining value from using the product you have created, then some of that value needs to be channeled into the maintenance and iteration of the product by investing in the people who use it, to support the products.

Data Skills for Better Decision-Making

There is a range of skills needed for anyone working with data in the modern working world. Being fluent with data involves a lot of phases, from understanding how to extract data from its source through visually communicating insights to the viewer. Teaching the full range of skills to everyone in your organization would be fantastic, but no one has infinite time and an unlimited training budget.

This section will cover what skills you need to consider for yourself and others and what level of expertise each person needs to have.

WHAT SKILLS?

For any discipline, the more skills you have, the better. Working with data is no different. After completing school, many people expect to have the core skills they need at work. Sadly, the prerequisite skills for data haven't traditionally been taught to an adequate level to use data effectively in most jobs. You and your organization will need to fill those skills gaps if you want to create more data-informed decisions.

Let's start at the foundational level of skills and work toward the more advanced.

Understanding outputs

Being able to interpret charts is the most foundational skill required when working with data products. Learning to read bar and line charts, scatterplots, and tables of data is vital to be able to interpret the parts of most data communications. If charts are built well using the pre-attentive attributes that power them, interpretation should be easy for the viewer.

The next skill built on this ability is combining insights from multiple sources to form a more contextualized view of the situation. If all the various charts are from the same communication, the author should have made this easier. If the charts are from multiple sources, there are a larger number of considerations you should take into account:

- The trustworthiness of the source

- The age of the data sources

- Any biases added by the authors of the work

- The purpose; why the communications were created

These factors will shape what you can take from the work and how much you can trust your interpretation. Learning how to question sources of data products happens naturally through exposure to working with data outputs, but can be supplemented with more traditional forms of learning such as reading books, watching tutorials, or attending classes.

Analysis

The next skill set required once you understand how to read and interpret others' outputs is to create your own analysis. Building your own analysis will require many of the skills covered in this book so far: asking the right questions, working directly with the data sources, and using your numerical skills to find ratios, variances, and outliers.

The skills required to conduct the analysis is one part; enacting that analysis is another. Building your experience of analyzing data sets will turn a skill set into a real capability. Many courses, books, and tutorials are available to teach the individual skills required to analyze data, but many overlook the importance of creating the space to practice and refine those skills.

Despite studying for an analytical academic degree and being a curious person by nature, only by conducting a range of data analyses did I (Carl) really hone the skills to be able to find insights in the data sets I had access to. I was very lucky that others in my organization created the opportunity for me to practice and develop my analytical abilities. If you are leading data projects, try to create opportunities for the people on your team to learn analytical skills and, further, to refine the skills they have learned through practice.

Communicating data

Once you have insightful findings, you will want to share them with your team, peers, and leadership. The best way to do this is by visualizing the data during your analysis. This way, once you make your findings, you can share these charts as the method of communicating your insights.

As with performing analysis, there is no single right or wrong way to communicate data. Visualizing data is a skill that requires practice and refinement; ensure that your ability to communicate it also improves over time. By starting with just single charts and slowly adding more complexity, through multiple charts and then interactivity, you will be able to share more complex messages with wider audiences. Many early pieces of data analysis will be *explanatory*. This means the analysis will communicate a detail regarding a specific question. As your skill set develops, you will likely be able to answer not just specific questions in a single communication but allow for users to explore the issue further themselves through introducing additional filters, interactivity, and alternate views for different levels of detail; this is called *exploratory* analysis.

One of the skills that everyone needs to learn is how to use the specific software your organization prefers to build data communications in. The fundamental skill of how to effectively communicate through visualizing the data is enacted only when using the software available to do so. In most organizations, you will not have free rein to choose which software you will use to form the communications. If you are leading a team or function, you should consider training in the visualization tool to empower people (and yourself) to be able to communicate what they need to.

Going beyond data analysis

For the most advanced analysis, you will need the most advanced skills. If you are to leverage new data sources, test hypotheses, and use predictive models, you will need a wide-ranging set of skills.

Only with a strong understanding of the data you are using and a clear objective can you begin to contemplate building predictive models to forecast results. You will need to have strong statistical skills to model the data and interpret the results of the models. Without these skills, you risk drawing false conclusions or developing models that don't accurately represent what you developed them for.

Creating strong analytical work is not just about building predictive models and all the prerequisites needed to run those models. Communicating the outputs to others is a key skill often overlooked when preparing data science teams to succeed. Due to the complexity of forming models, clear communications and the ability to simplify complex concepts are required to help stakeholders understand how much they should rely on the outputs.

Many skills are required but, thankfully, you don't need to develop all of these skills in every employee in your organization to be successful in developing greater data-informed decision-making. Having a few specialists focused on working on key initiatives normally meets the needs of most organizations.

SKILLS FOR WHOM?

Dividing your peers into three groups can help you understand what skills you need to ensure each individual has to help them make data-informed decisions:

Viewers

> Anyone who consumes visual data products needs to be able to understand how to interpret the charts and analyses created by others. Understanding how the data has been sourced will also allow the viewers to question bias or potential gaps in the data.

Editors

> Editors don't just view the products of others, but make changes to tailor the data products to their own needs. This may involve changing filters applied to data sources or combining different charts to tell an alternate analysis to what has already been produced. Their skill set will need to include some analytical skills as well as communication skills.

Creators

> The creators are those who build data products from scratch. They will have an excellent understanding of how to interpret others' work, analyze new data sets, and communicate the findings found from them. The creators might be able to work on data science projects once they have understood the business challenges and verified the data sources that might answer the questions posed. Building predictive models comes once a solid understanding is in place, but does require statistical skills and an understanding of predictive methodologies.

Determining who fits in each category and what skill gaps there are entails work in its own right. Interviewing people about their roles, needs, and existing data skills is a key way to form a view over what data knowledge and skills your organization has compared to what it requires.

Summary

Data can be intimidating when you first work with it, due to many factors. From reading this chapter, you should feel more comfortable in your understanding of what data is, the terminology to describe its different features, and what you can produce with it. Ultimately, by starting to work with data, you will not only enhance your own data fluency but will likely improve others' skill levels and awareness as you share the outputs you and your teams create. There are many skills you would need were you to try to do everything within a single project; but please let us reassure you that there are very few of those unicorns who can be an expert at all the different aspects and tools that are required to work with data.

You will likely need a team of people to deliver the different components of each data project. The next chapter will take you through the different products you might create at each step when undertaking a project involving data.

The Building Blocks of a Data Analysis System

Data projects can be complicated, but they needn't be. There are infinite outcomes possible with data. Knowing the different stages of data projects will enable you to fragment the complexity and make projects more manageable. The aim of this chapter is for you to be able to play an active role in any data project and help guide it through to delivery.

This chapter will work through the common stages of a data project:

- Sourcing data through extraction from your systems or acquisition from third parties

- Storing data at all project stages and for the long term

- Curating and enriching data

- Exploring and analyzing data sets

- Sharing the data products created by your project

The overarching theme of this chapter will be how important it is to identify what problem you are trying to solve with a data project. Focusing on the problem is key, as you are likely to come across roadblocks and will need different options as you create the solutions needed. Allowing yourself the opportunity to pivot as you learn from the data and analysis you are working with is key. This is better than staying steadfast in what you originally set out in a requirements document a long time ago.

Data Extraction and Acquisition

It may go without saying, but you can't have a data project without having or thinking about getting hold of data. There are three main ways to get data: extraction, acquisition, and creation. Here, we will focus on the first two: extraction and acquisition. Each method of collecting data has its own challenges, but by undertaking either, you are unlocking the opportunity to make better-informed decisions.

DATA EXTRACTION

While search engines help to find external sources of data, you will need to rely on your own network and supportive colleagues in IT to guide you to the relevant internal sources. To begin to find out what data might need to be extracted for your analysis, you will need to find what operational systems create or capture the data you need. Once you've identified the systems, you can then work with IT to understand what underlying data sets have been created and how they can be accessed. If you are lucky enough, the data you want will already have been extracted for analysis. If not, you will need to understand what data is stored and can be accessed.

Taking samples of the data fields from the source will help you understand what you might need and what you do not. Querying operational systems to extract vast amounts of data can impact the operational system's performance. Using small samples can tell you about what transformations and cleaning will have to occur if you were to extract larger volumes of data. The clearer and more detailed you can be about the data you want, the more easily your IT teams can schedule with confidence when they can get access and how much effort it will take.

With an increasing reliance on cloud-hosted, third-party software and solutions, gaining access to the underlying data sets can be more challenging. You might expect that, as it is your organization's data the third party is hosting, you should be able to access it easily, but that isn't always the case. Unless there is data access granted contractually, you might be left without analytical access.

Another decision you will need to make is how your data set will be processed when you add new records. The nature of the contents of your data and how the source system holds it will heavily guide this decision. There are two main ways this handled:

Full refresh
> This involves deleting the original data and reloading all the data. This is largely superfluous if the original data doesn't change and only new records are added. If the records might have been updated and you only want to see the most recent values, then a full refresh is the best approach.

Incremental refresh
> This involves having an ordinal field, a data field with an inherent order, as with dates, in the data that can be used to identify when the last data load occurred so all subsequent records can then be added. This method of extracting data is more efficient, as you're not reloading unchanged data.

Once you have access to the data, you can start planning how you'll process and prepare it for analysis. The ETL methodology involves making any manipulations you need before you load the data into your analytical database. This takes more planning and a clearer understanding of what you will need in the long term.

The ELT alternate option is more aligned with cloud computing, which allows for more scalable processing. As data processing needs increase and data sets become larger, the flexibility of cloud computing helps meet the changing needs. More processing can be added on demand, rather than having to buy and install additional physical computer servers as with on-premises setups.

One of the most significant benefits of ELT is that the raw data set is stored, so it can be manipulated in different ways as business needs change. This allows for a more future-proofed approach to working with data, as you can change the structure, clean, and filter the data without fear of removing anything from the original data set. The ETL method may remove data points during the initial setup that become important in the future, because they aren't initially deemed relevant.

DATA ACQUISITION

Data acquisition involves purchasing or taking on data from a third-party supplier. With more companies offering feeds of data through APIs or as a paid service, this endeavor is one you are likely to encounter.

The first challenge with data acquisition is often finding not just any data source that suits your need but the best source of data for the need. It doesn't matter if you are spending money to acquire the data or getting it for free, you will still be using organizational resources to set up the feeds, so you need to ensure the data itself is right for what you need.

One of the organizational resources you'll be using is time. So how much time is the right amount to expend on a project? Sourcing data should be proportional to the potential length of its use. If you want a few values to support a single point in a one-and-done PowerPoint, then finding accurate data is important, but finding a source that will keep the data up-to-date is less of a requirement. If the data will power a longer-term solution, it is more proportionate to spend a greater amount of time checking for alternate sources that might better fit the needs of your project. You won't always know how much effort it will take to acquire the data, but by running quick tests, you will quickly be able to learn about potential time-consuming challenges ahead.

Bringing the data into your organization isn't always as simple as just downloading a file from the data provider's website. Data sets can be gigantic. If the data updates frequently too, you will need to invest in setting up a data pipeline that can perform the following functions:

- Provide security for you and the provider
- Handle the volume of data
- Handle the velocity of data
- Handle the variety of data received

A *data pipeline* refers to the process of taking the data from its source or provider and loading it into storage. Data pipelines can also contain the transformational steps that convert the data into a shape ready for analysis.

The last point here is one that is less frequently considered but is an expensive oversight if made. The supplier of data sets rarely makes a data set just for your specific need. This means that the structure, filename, or data field names may change as the supplier updates what they have available. If your data pipeline and storage solution is built just to handle the original qualities of the data, you will find the pipeline may break and fail, rendering your acquisition useless.

Building a suitable data pipeline requires specialist knowledge of how to work with data pipelines and workflows, as well as how to navigate completing this task in your organization specifically. For example, creating access points in your organization's security firewalls is just one of the many tasks required if you repeatedly absorb large amounts of data.

One way that you gain access to the third-party systems hosting your data is through APIs. APIs have become key elements in making data available from transactional systems to import to your data storage or analytical platforms. APIs are designed to allow computer programs to communicate with each other rather than delivering data directly to end users. This is why APIs are used to pipe data from source systems to analytical platforms. Like any technology, APIs have developed over time to become easier to use as well as having richer functionality. If you are working on a data project requiring APIs, you are likely to need a specialist unless you have a lot of experience coding your own solutions. A key component of modern data projects is having programmers who can help you understand the possibilities with the APIs available from the systems you need data from.

You'll also need to consider whether you need the acquired data set to update. If you do, you will need to understand when the data set is likely to update and how you will recognize it has changed. You will rarely want to delete an acquired data set and just upload the data afresh. Therefore, it is important to recognize the fields in the acquired data set that will change so you can determine when new records are available. The documentation often supplied with APIs illustrates what to look for. However, using other sources of data, e.g., *web scraping,* or copying data from an internet page, won't likely have this in place. Web scraping can be done through many specialist tools, such as Web Queries in Microsoft Excel, or the *IMPORTHTML* function in Google Sheets, to load data from tables found on websites. You may need to work with the data provider to understand the frequency of available updates and how to recognize when you need to gain fresh information.

Acquiring a data set from a third-party provider requires you to depend on the provider's organization. Depending on the importance of the data set to your organization, you may want to audit the provider's long-term capability to support the production of the data set. If this acquired data set becomes a key part of your organization's processes, then you will need to ensure you have agreements in place to maintain the flow of data. Where you can't form those agreements, you are opening yourself up to long-term risk that the data-driven processes may break.

Acquiring a data set means you are just as responsible for the use of the data as you are for the sources you create yourself. This means you will need to ensure the data set adheres to all relevant regulations and is governed carefully. When acquiring a data set, it can be challenging to trace back to the subject of the data to ensure they have given their permission for its collection and use. This may be a time-consuming process, but it is important to ensure that your organization is protected from long-term impacts of data misuse, such as litigation and fines from regulators.

The final challenge you need to consider when acquiring data is the potential for the provider to introduce bias into the data set. In "Key Features of Data" on page 18, we introduced you to the importance of questioning a data set. Here, we'll look at how bias can creep into data sets. Researching the organization providing the data to see if there are any potential political, economic, social, or religious biases is an important step that is often overlooked. If you assume a data set represents the full population but it represents only a limited segment of society, you risk forming poor and misleading conclusions. Potential biases can be introduced in a plethora of ways; a few are listed here:

- Limiting who data is collected from
- Filtering out certain values
- Poorly termed questions
- Collating biased sources to form the new data source

Fixing bias in data sets you don't own is very difficult, so you either need to factor in those biases when you use the data or find alternative sources.

Data Storage Logic and Terminology

Once you have access to the data you require for your project, the next step is to work out where you are going to store it. With an array of options open to you, this may seem trickier than you might first imagine. Your organization may limit some of these options by having guidelines you'll be required to adhere to or only providing the ability to access a restricted range of tools. If there isn't an established method or technology for data storage, you'll need to assess what is right for your organization and your project. Each option will have a number of pros and cons, so let's look at each in turn.

TYPES

Like everything else you will encounter with data, the business problem you are solving will shape the data set you need. The shape of your data, the number of rows, and the structure of your data will influence your storage options.

We can't detail all the specifics of each situation you'll come across, but we will highlight the key differences and where one solution becomes no longer feasible and you'll need to consider another.

You may find the data stores you have access to can absorb the data sources you create through your data project, but the question you need to ask yourself is, "should they"? For decades, organizations have squeezed the last bit of capacity, memory, or capability out of many data sources to avoid systematic change that would substantially affect existing solutions and all the data products that are linked to them. If you are creating a brand-new project that needs to last, it's key to ensure the data source is scalable to the solution at hand and meets the users' needs, without leaving them with a spinning loading icon on their screens. We'll look at the options that are available to you next.

Spreadsheets

Although many data professionals would argue that spreadsheets are not a strategic data storage platform, they still play a key part in holding important data sets for most organizations, as discussed in "The shape of data" on page 25. The flexibility spreadsheets offer ensures that they can meet the needs of many people. Cells can hold any data types you want, data doesn't have to be structured in specific ways, and files can be updated by simply overwriting the values that exist in the file already. The flexibility of spreadsheets can allow for a number of data products to be created from them.

One advantage of spreadsheets is that the source data and output are held together, often on separate tabs but still within the same file. This can make it easier to question how the data has led to the results of the analysis. Many consultants build financial models in spreadsheets, as they are easier to share with their clients and can have their client's data quickly added. If these models are to be used repeatedly, then other tools might be preferable, but the bespoke nature of this work means that spreadsheets are still the tool of choice for many.

Yet, the flexibility offered by spreadsheets is actually the reason why they are a poor choice for data storage. Analytical tools expect to find just one data type in each column. As a spreadsheet doesn't have to structure the same type of data in a data field or with the name in the top row of the data set, many business intelligence tools will struggle to read the data held within them. Data points can be easily overwritten by clicking a cell and pushing keys. This can lead to errors when using the spreadsheet with other tools or in the analysis itself.

If data is held in columns with names at the top of each field, you may still struggle due to the limitation of rows a spreadsheet can have. Microsoft Excel has a limit of 1,048,576 rows, after which you cannot add any additional data. This sounds like a lot, and it is, but with larger data sets becoming increasingly common, spreadsheets often cannot handle the full data set. This means files have to be fragmented, creating more complexity when trying to work with them.

Sharing spreadsheet files can be both a blessing and a curse when it comes to data storage. The ease of sharing spreadsheets can mean data is easier to use, as permissions to more secure data stores don't need to be granted before access can be gained. The curse comes from the same scenario. As data sets can be passed between colleagues, or even externally, control of the data set is instantly lost. The implications of this include the following:

- Losing track of the source of the information as it gets passed between more people
- Inability to update the data set if the original source is lost
- Data security not possible, as it relies on others not passing the data on
- Difficulty in tracking data use to meet the subject's rights to control the use of their own data

Without excellent version control of the spreadsheet, it's easy for others to change the original data set. This could change the findings someone would make from analyzing the data set or result in them missing out on updated data. If spreadsheets are used to store data in your data project, you need to be making that choice with careful consideration of the previously mentioned factors.

Databases

Many of the factors disadvantageous to the use of spreadsheets can be fixed by using databases. *Databases* are software solutions designed to ingest, process, store, and output data. Databases are loaded onto data servers that are designed especially for the tasks they will undertake. Servers are still computers, but they have much more storage and computational processing power than your laptop or desktop computer. Databases are therefore designed for the specific purposes that you will care about when working on data projects and considering what storage options to take.

Many databases traditionally use a coding language called *Structured Query Language* (SQL) to allow you to work with the data held within them. SQL is a comprehensive language that can allow you to create, update, query, and delete database tables. SQL is widely known amongst most analysts, but it is not often taught to non-data specialists. This means accessing the data held within databases can prove to be difficult for many people.

In "Going beyond files" on page 29, we introduced you to databases and the ways they hold the data within systems. Let's get into more detail about how relational databases break data sets into different types of tables. *Fact tables* hold the measures of the data set, and the commonly repeated dimensions are held in *dimension tables*. Dimension tables keep the names of the categorical data points alongside a numerical identifier. As numerical identifiers are quicker to process and smaller to store, dimension tables help to reduce the overall size and complexity involved when processing data queries. As dimensional values are often repeated across data sets, they are held once in the dimension tables, and then the identifiers are used in the fact tables.

The approach taken to organize fact and dimension tables can take a few shapes. The most common you will encounter are star and snowflake schemas (Figure 3-1). Both schemas are named after the configuration created when the tables within it are mapped out on a page:

Star schema
> A star schema has many dimension tables that connect to the fact table, like the light beams from the center of a star.

Snowflake schema
> In nature, a snowflake's nucleus has dendrites emerging from it that then have further smaller dendrites emerging from them. The data snowflake is named as are detailed dimension tables and can be joined onto other dimension tables before linking to the fact table.

While it is unlikely you will personally decide on the schema type if you have a DBA looking after the service, you may need to understand which has been used to structure your data within a database. *Database administrator* is a common role you will have in an IT team in medium and large organizations to maintain and optimize the updates and storage.

As the user of a database, you have to consider the complexity you are leaving for yourself in the future and your fellow users of the data. Snowflake schemas can be easier to maintain, utilize less space, and have fewer data integrity issues, as elements are stored at an appropriate level of detail as to how many variables there are for each category. A star schema requires fewer joins to combine the different tables and with fewer joins will process the queries faster. Therefore, one of the factors that determines what schema type might be best is the skills of the users. The deciding factor of which schema type should be used is likely the predominant one used in your organization to date.

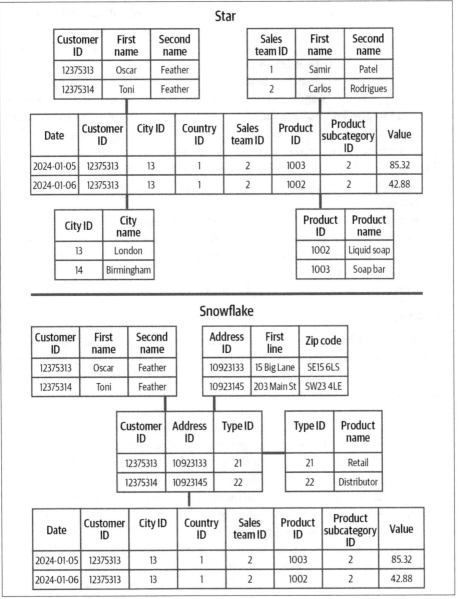

Figure 3-1. Star and snowflake schemas (a larger version of this figure is available at https://oreil.ly/HAjLk)

Multiple databases can exist alongside each other on the same computer; these are called *data servers*. Data servers that are architected for analysis are classed as *data warehouses*. With so much data held together, database software is designed to allow for control of access permissions. When working on data projects, understanding who needs, or can have, access to certain data fields or records is an important part of the project. If you restrict access too much, your users of the output might not be able to find what they need. If you don't put enough controls in place, you may be at risk of revealing data the end user might not be legally allowed to see.

Databases have much richer functionality and more powerful querying performance than spreadsheets and other data file storage options. With this richness comes an overhead to plan and manage your data, as you can't create, edit, and use databases spontaneously. When you are conducting analysis and developing data products from database sources, you want the data structure to remain stable. Planning the structure and access you will require from your database will make or break many data projects, as you will not be able to change the schemas rapidly if the underlying data or requirements change.

You might be thinking databases are the right storage solution for nearly all scenarios, as they are specifically designed for many circumstances, but you'd be wrong. The growth of data volume, velocity, and variety has challenged databases, as many software solutions weren't designed with the flexibility and scale required to work with the data produced by more modern applications.

Data lakes

Data lakes offered part of the solution to many of the challenges that databases were not designed to address. Primarily, a data lake takes its name from its ability to absorb and store a vast variety and volume of data from all types of different sources producing data. While databases can store only structured data, data lakes can also store unstructured data.

Unstructured data refers to data sets that do not have a defined structure of rows, columns, or relationships, as seen in databases. Unstructured data can include files, text, media, or sensor data. The benefit of data lakes holding unstructured data is that it doesn't have to be processed and transformed before being stored. This means data can be absorbed into storage much faster, allowing much more data to be captured than if transformation had to occur first. Web application data, social media, or any digital click can all be captured as data streams in.

As you analyze data and your data project evolves, being able to iterate what you are looking for and how it is held is important so that you can gain the biggest benefit possible. As soon as you begin to analyze data, you will start learning and therefore are likely to ask different, more advanced questions. Data lakes allow for all data to be absorbed without specifying the schema. As you analyze data from a data lake, you will form the schema required to meet your need. This contrasts with having to specify it up front as you would if your data project was going to use a database as a storage solution.

Just dumping data sets into a data lake isn't a sufficient storage approach. You will need to catalog the data being stored in a data lake for potential users to know what they have access to. *Data catalogs* contain metadata (the data about the data) and search functionalities to allow users to go and find what they are looking for. Data catalogs have become software products in their own right, which means you will have another vendor to work with unless your organization has one in place.

Data lakes can require a different skill set than traditional analysts have. As files are unstructured, data fields and records cannot be referenced in queries as you'd expect with SQL. R and Python, along with other programming languages, have become much more common in organizations to help work with and extract the value from data held in data lakes.

For the majority of the people in your organization and the business intelligence tools they utilize, databases are still required too.

Data lakehouses

Data lakehouses have begun to bring together the benefits of structured databases and the flexibility of data lakes into a single domain. Data lakehouses have been invented to create a single location that utilizes the benefits of both data storage methodologies.

By creating a single solution, the same underlying data set can be explored as you would a data lake, but they also have a developed database schema. Data lakehouses have also brought in many of the data management features found in databases, as they were missing in the data lake setup. This combination of structured, semi-structured, and unstructured data has allowed a wide range of data workers to get what they need from the same data sets.

As data storage solutions develop, you may need to rely on what you already have in place in your organization. If you do get to choose to start from scratch, a data lakehouse may offer the best of both worlds, but solutions are still developing and maturing.

LOCATION OF DATA SERVERS

Choosing the technological model for your data project's storage is the first step, but where you host that solution is another key consideration. Throughout the 2010s, the emergence of cloud computing became a real option for many organizations to host their data. Before this, on-premises hosting of data servers was the only permissible option. Your own decision about where you host your data servers will be largely dependent on what model your organization runs on.

Understanding the benefits and drawbacks of both options is an important factor when sourcing data from others as well as storing your own.

On-premises

Hosting your data sources *on-premises* means owning and running the data servers yourself within a building your organization operates. This used to be the standard for a number of reasons, but primarily security. By hosting the data servers within your own buildings, they were likely to be within your own organization's firewall. A *firewall* is a security device separating your organization's computer network from the public. Firewalls filter network traffic and only allow permitted access. Before cloud computing became more standard, trying to get permission and then establish an access point through your organization's firewall was a time-consuming process, as it increased the risk of hacking attempts and care needed to be taken.

Having the data server within your firewall made connecting to other on-premises hosted data sources much easier. The majority of systems that you would require data from or other data servers you would need to access were all on-premises, so it was a relatively simple decision to continue that trend. With the rise of cloud-hosted applications and data sources, this is no longer the case. However, there were other benefits of on-premises hosting:

Control of your applications

Version control of the applications used to be very tightly controlled to ensure any update wouldn't inadvertently interfere with other applications or data products. By hosting the application on-premises, you are responsible for updates, so can choose what gets installed and when. This means you can avoid peak usage times and/or key reporting periods, like the ends of quarters.

Up-front cost

With on-premises software, the licensing model has traditionally been focused on higher up-front cost with a smaller residual amount to cover version updates and product support. This can be a benefit wherein you are able to request higher values as part of the initial project and then factor in the maintenance costs as a continuous operational expenditure.

The major drawback of on-premises solutions is that everything happens on servers you acquire, manage, and maintain. There are a few impacts to this point; firstly, you need to size the capacity and performance requirements very carefully at the outset of a project to ensure the data servers will be capable of storing and processing the data generated by the data products. As I've mentioned, many data projects evolve over time as insight is gained while working on a project, which creates more traction and users. Secondly, if data is created and stored as part of your data project, this volume will likely grow over time, meaning that you don't use the full resources of the data server you need to establish for a long time. This is where on-premises solutions are seen as costly and wasteful compared to their cloud-hosted counterparts. The final impact is needing to have the architects to design the data servers and maintenance skills to fix inevitable issues when they occur.

Cloud

Cloud solutions were created to answer many of the impacts felt from hosting everything on-premises yourself. *Cloud computing* refers to an external network of servers that are often owned and operated by a third-party organization like Microsoft Azure, Google Cloud Platform, or Amazon Web Services. Your organization or the country you are operating in may limit which cloud provider you can use due to security concerns or fear of other countries holding sensitive data. Cloud computing providers offer huge amounts of potential to scale up, and can back increased capacity and processing of data, often on a moment's notice. The most significant drawback of on-premises solutions is their fixed and preset amount of capacity; cloud computing solves this.

Cloud networks use the internet to connect their servers together to create potentially huge arrays of servers to draw resources from. These networks create cheaper options than on-premises solutions by working at enormous scales to generate economies of scale. For many key applications, your organization will likely run backup systems to allow the applications to still run if there are any issues in the original setup. Cloud providers can offer this more cheaply, as most of the failover options will not need to be running at any given time, so the processing power can be shared amongst their setups.

With more data sources and applications being hosted on the cloud, having your data servers in the cloud will make accessing the data much easier. If your data servers were on-premises but relied on data sources on cloud networks, you'd need to open access points in your firewall. Apart from reducing the effort to connect to cloud-based data sources, cloud networks have other benefits:

Managed updates
> Having data servers set up for you is not the only cloud option to consider. Many solutions you may have to consider will include fully managed systems that operate in the cloud. This means all updates will be completed for you.

Cheaper up-front licensing
> With the ability to scale up and down on cloud-hosted solutions, license fee models have changed to be more focused on usage rather than heavy up-front costs. This model means that as your organization uses the data solution more, your costs will increase. However, if the solution is not adopted or used widely, you

won't have paid as much for the licensing costs as you would for the on-premises solution. This reduces the overall project investment risk.

Whichever location you choose to deploy your data resources to, you will need to manage the data stores that build over time. Data projects need to consider their long-term management and put the relevant controls in place.

Data Enrichment and Curation

Data sources can be very valuable, but only once they are well-structured are they understandable and easily managed. When data is stored, it hasn't necessarily been structured, understood, or managed to this point. This section will look at how data sources can be made more valuable by combining different data sources together to create a more holistic view.

Once your data sources are developed, you need to consider how to maintain them to keep them as valuable as when they are created. Managing data sources takes effort, but when done well can save a lot of time and (re)work as the data sources are applied for alternative uses. Providing data management of and governance controls on data sets can mean the difference between data being used because it is trusted or neglected as an unreliable mess.

As you factor these management aspects into how your project's data is kept and maintained, you can then add a final layer by curating the data to make it more usable. Cataloging data has spawned a whole set of software products to help with this task. Documenting the metadata, the data about the data, helps make your data source be discoverable and usable by the widest audience possible.

DATA TRANSFORMATION VERSUS ENRICHMENT

If your organization's primary data sources have traditionally been spreadsheets, you have probably spent a lot of time transforming data. Reshaping data to prepare it for use with a business intelligence tool, or just analysis within the spreadsheet software itself, can be a time-consuming, thankless task. There is little recognition from the audience of the data output regarding how much transformational work may have been involved in producing the data product. Many executives are used to just asking for the information they want without understanding the time and effort it takes to wrangle the necessary data points to respond to their request.

Transforming data involves changing the shape of the data source and often involves cleaning individual data fields. With spreadsheets, you will have probably learned how to use CTRL+C and CTRL+V to copy and paste data from some cells to others. But with modern tools, there are easier ways to create and automate these processes. Automation is important to remove the effort involved in repeated, manual steps. If these processes are left as manual work, the repetitive nature frequently leads to mistakes by the person undertaking the task, no matter how dutiful they are. Trust me on this, I've run a team whose majority of work fell into this category, and they were great, but mistakes still crept in.

Automation of data transformation is often built in what is classed as a workflow. *Workflows* are so called as they do their work by sending the data through a series of transformational steps. Although workflows can be scripted, many tools, like Tableau Prep and Alteryx, offer drag-and-drop interactions to allow users to build the workflow that iterates their processes best, until they have made all the necessary changes, without having to find the relevant instruction in a block of code.

Enrichment differs from transformation, as it involves adding data fields and points to provide additional context or detail to a data source. This is where data sources can really be made more valuable by combining them in a way that no other organizational system can do. Joining data tables together can add useful data points, establishing reasons for why the records are what they are. Let's look at a few examples:

Patient histories at a hospital

Adding demographic information from patients' addresses' local areas might help provide insight into some of the causes for visits to the facility. Maybe financial hardship is leading to a poor diet and causing poorer health.

Customer purchases

Adding data on market share for your organization sourced from research companies can help promote understanding as to whether higher sales are a result of your organization's performance or are similar to wider market trends.

Farming crop yields

Adding weather data may help farmers understand the reasons for changes in their crop yields.

Creating an enriched data source might mean that you need to replicate the data source and therefore double the data storage cost. This doesn't have to be the case, as you can create views in databases that only reference the location of the original data source. When they are used, they have all the join logic built in to make them as easy to use as a database table. Unless the naming conventions in the database are very clear, you might not even realize when you're using a view instead of a table.

With the vast amount of data organizations have built up over time, enriching data can be a key part of turning an unwieldy volume of data into something usable by everyone. Many data projects have been conducted just to build richer data sources, allowing analysts and domain experts to ask more detailed questions than ever before.

Once data sources have been created, they need to be maintained and governed to ensure they remain accurate and up to date.

DATA QUALITY AND GOVERNANCE

Once you have formed a data source, you need to ensure it remains relevant and reliable to the situation it covers. Data can quickly become out of date, be updated incorrectly, or be copied multiple times, creating a challenge when it comes to understanding which to use and the differences between them. Let's look at how each of these can occur and the resulting effects:

Out of date

> If the workflow that forms your data source isn't designed with source data updates in mind, you are in danger of the records becoming out of date. This means any new data points won't be automatically added to the data source. You could be missing out on seeing changes in customer behavior or issues arising that could be easily seen if the data is refreshed.

Updated incorrectly

> You need to ensure data source updates happen correctly. When you update data, you are likely to conduct either a full refresh or an incremental refresh. A full refresh deletes all the current records in your set and replaces them with all the data in the data source at that time. An incremental refresh will upload only new records in the data set. If data field names or data types have changed, then your refresh may not run correctly, leaving no or incorrect data.

Multiple copies

> The final challenge is ensuring people aren't forming their own versions of the data source. This might involve adding data fields, filtering out records, or using older versions of the data source. When these copies are employed by others instead of the true data source, inadvertent errors are introduced into the decision-making process.

For decades, the existence of multiple copies of data has been among the largest concerns for most organizations. Retaining multiple copies wastes expensive storage space. Most organizations now focus on the concept of the "single source of the truth," or *golden source*. This concept makes sense, as things like financial information reported to the stock market, the volume of products required for the next quarter, or the number of complaints received all exemplify key pieces of information that your company will require to make sound decisions; therefore, having one consistent value is very important.

The single-source concept has been taken too far, in our opinion. The concept overlooks the fact that data from the same source may need to be treated differently by different business domains. Let's take sales data as an example of why you might want different versions of the same data, sometimes known as different *cuts* of data:

Sales

When dealing with business-to-business transactions, the sales team will want to know when the sale has been recorded and when the invoice has been paid. Only then do most sales commissions pay out. Their role requires a fine level of granularity: each row of data is likely to be an individual transaction.

Marketing

Marketing will want to know the data at a less granular level. They will want to understand, for example, which campaign led to a sale. Did the sale originate from an email campaign, or was it a discounted sale resulting from the Black Friday campaign?

Logistics

This team will need to know when a sale is made to adjust stock levels. There will be a more significant product and timing focus on this data set, with records of sales that haven't been fulfilled yet included.

Each of these data sets should be enriched with different data fields to enable each domain to answer their own questions. If you had all of these fields in a single data set, it would require it to be a very wide data source to include all the data fields. When data is held at different levels of granularity, the data sources have to be different as well, as each row will represent something very different. There is nothing wrong with this approach, but you must ensure the data can be traced back to the raw sales transaction. These sales transactions have to be stored only once but need to be available for different purposes, in multiple ways. This allows the data to be reconciled if there are variances that lead to potential confusion or misreporting.

Allowing for multiple views of the same underlying data source can create challenges with governing the data. It's vital to ensure that each cut of the data meets legal requirements for storing, updating, and deleting the data to remain within the terms of use. When a customer ends their relationship with a firm, they have the right to have their data deleted, but this is harder to achieve if a number of original sources of the data have to be identified first. Using a single underlying data source to power and update the views is the easiest way to achieve this.

The differing views of the data can pose challenges as to whether the data is still being used for the purposes specified when it was collected and its use permitted by the subjects of the data. If you have produced data products that you want to share with other departments for reasons beyond analysis, you will need to approach this care to ensure the data is used correctly. For example, if the actuarial department wants to use a data set you've collected from a survey on product concepts but it already has data on the respondents' family setup to update policy pricing, this shouldn't be allowed.

Governing data sources has become more challenging, but with strong data management guidelines to reduce the copying of data sources, this can become much easier to achieve.

CURATING DATA

Once you have stored your data, you won't gain any value from it sitting in a repository unused. Curating data sources involves making the data sources available to those who can make use of them. If you work in a small organization, you might be able to talk to potential users of your data set directly. However, as soon as your organization grows its number of employees towards 100, it becomes difficult to guide each person as to what data sources are available and where they will find them. Making metadata available and searchable in catalogs will help the data sources be used.

Metadata

Metadata is often defined as the data about the data. The information captured can be anything about the data source that helps describe what it is and why it has been created. Elements of metadata can include the following:

- Data source type

- File size

- Creation date and time

- Update date and time

- Creator

- Source of the data

There are other details that can also be classed as metadata, such as structural metadata. *Structural metadata* describes the format of the data source in terms of the columns, data types of the values, and rows held within it. Understanding what the data structure is helps identify whether the data source will help the user gain what they need. Being clear on what each record represents in the data set, also known as the *granularity* of the data, will help the data source be interpreted and used correctly. In database tables, structural metadata also includes which fields are keys and indexes. These factors help you to link together useful tables by joining different tables together carefully.

Catalogs

Data catalogs have become increasingly important as the variety of data sets has grown in every organization. The traditional way to find the data source you needed required knowing who to ask. For the most part, database administrators, the people who are responsible for structuring and running data environments, were the guides to the data, both in terms of what was available and how to get access. Within smaller organizations, this is still possible, but for multinational organizations just finding a DBA is a tough enough challenge, let alone finding the person who knows where to actually find the data you want.

Data cataloging tools have become a key part of data platforms, as they are now the guides to what data exists, where it resides, and what it means. Most data catalog tools will scan through databases and data sources to identify what metadata exists and make this information searchable. Many data storage tools have some level of ability to search within them, but data catalogs have the advantage of being able to work across multiple databases and storage solutions at the same time, creating a more comprehensive overview.

Data curation can easily be overlooked. Understanding what tools and techniques your organization uses to make data sources more easily shared and understood is an important step in enabling your organization to make data-informed decisions. This helps people find the right data to answer their questions, rather than having to spend time searching for someone to guide them to a particular source for each question they have.

Data Exploration and Analysis

Once you have found the right data, developed data sources from those data sets, and created meaning from the data, you then get to the most valuable part of the process, developing analyses and insight. The process of forming insights first involves data exploration to understand what the data represents, how complete the data source is, and what problems can be answered by the data.

Turning data into information and insight is a skill that isn't taught widely enough, but it can be fostered in most people. Encouraging everyone to work with data is one of the major threads running through this book. Ensuring that this is the case for the subject matter experts, or domain experts as we've also been referring to them, who work in the area your project addresses is key to your organization taking full advantage of its data resources. Using tools that allow SMEs to leverage their knowledge no matter their level of data fluency is vital.

If you don't put the data in the hands of the SMEs in the organization, they will only be able to use generic overviews of the data. These overall views will likely be simple counts that are unlikely to unearth the true value in the data. After all, to deliver a great data project, you'll want to garner the most value from the data possible.

Let's address what data exploration involves before looking at how you can empower your SMEs to explore your organization's data sets.

WHAT IS DATA EXPLORATION?

Data exploration involves profiling the data source to understand not just what fields you have within it, but also the range of categorical values, the date range covered, and the distribution of key measures. This is the first step of turning the data into information and then, more importantly, insights.

When using a data source for the first time, it's always a good idea to profile the data set. Without profiling the data, you run the risk of making unfounded assumptions. Data profiling allows you to test what you expect to see in the data against what is actually occurring. Take Figure 3-2 as an example. If your business is seasonal, i.e., has higher sales in one part of the year than others, the chart looks as you'd expect, with higher numbers of orders in the final quarter of each year. However, if your expectation is that each month will have similar numbers of orders, you'll want to dig deeper into why there are differences in the number of orders per month. System outages, data pipeline errors, or even accidental changes to the data source can all create gaps in the data that can lead to incorrect conclusions.

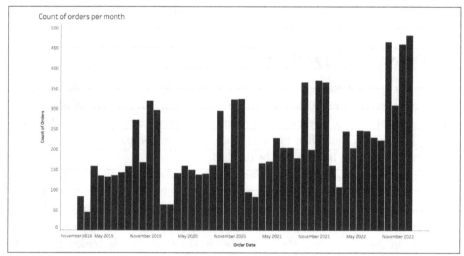

Figure 3-2. Data profiling (a larger version of this figure is available at https://oreil.ly/UJpPI)

There are a number of approaches you can take to profile a data set. Here are a few aspects to consider:

- Counts of unique values
- Number of records for each variable within a field

- Measurements of deviation between data points

- Measurements of excessive data points (i.e., anything above 100%)

When you are conducting this exploration, you might choose to use just summary statistics such as mean, standard deviation, and other statistical measures, but by visualizing the data, you are much more likely to reveal additional insights such as outliers and trends. Figure 3-3 demonstrates the use of box plots to look at the distribution of state sales values for a retailer.

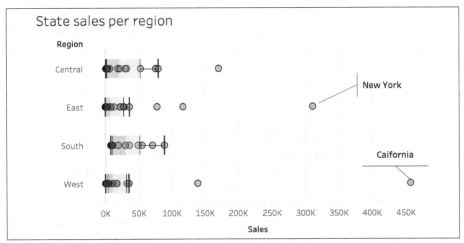

Figure 3-3. Visualizing variance of values (a larger version of this figure is available at https://oreil.ly/Qb3ZS)

Humans have an excellent ability to see patterns in images. Visualizing the data makes it much easier for people to see outliers and trends in your data. We don't need to tell you which states are outliers in each region in Figure 3-3, as the visualization makes that clear. Very few people working in your organization will have a strong understanding of standard deviation, p-values, or other summary statistics. By visualizing the data, you can utilize pre-attentive attributes to demonstrate distributions and strengths of correlations within the data more easily to people who don't have deep statistical understanding. Charts like box plots aren't instantly understandable for the majority of an audience, but the key features can be quickly annotated and shared.

There isn't a clear distinction between exploration and analytics. By starting with data exploration, you will quickly begin to create beneficial analyses and insights.

CREATING ANALYTICAL OUTPUTS

Your data project may create a number of useful data products, from those set out in the requirements documents to those that emerge as helpful byproducts of the project.

People beyond the original requestor will frequently use the data source(s) you create at the different stages of the project as the primary or supplementary data source for their own work. As you acquire or extract data and before you transform it to the requirements indicated, you will want to store this data source for future use in its rawer form. This means any transformation you perform won't restrict others from using other parts of the data source. Documenting the data source so others know what might be gained from it is key to it being used in the future. There are many ways to document data, but as discussed in "Curating Data Sources" on page 37, specialist data cataloging tools are becoming increasingly popular to do this.

Visualizing data is useful for data exploration and can form the first analytical output for your own use. As visualization is such an effective medium to communicate data, these visual explorations are useful to share directly with others. Without visualizing the data, sharing the insights you've found with others takes more time and effort. Visualized charts can be shared with SMEs directly to facilitate them adding their experience to the data to form richer insights.

Much of the basic reporting that has been traditionally formed when running a data project should really be only the first step. Throughout this book, we've highlighted the benefits of learning and iterating. Basic reports are created to report standard key performance indicators (KPIs). If the data originates from an updating source, these reports should be scheduled to refresh frequently. Microsoft SSRS, IBM's Cognos, and SAP BusinessObjects are some of many reporting tools that first offered automated reporting beyond what Excel made available to its users. These tools were usually owned and operated by centralized IT teams, which restricted some of the applications of domain expertise.

It's easy to develop a data product and just focus on the technical aspects of the project. Neglecting the organizational problem or challenges you are attempting to resolve with the data project is where a number of projects can go off course. The domain experts should be brought into the analytical process early to ensure their knowledge and experience are used alongside the data. Involving SMEs makes the solution much more likely to impact the problem as intended from the project's outset. Creating data sources that can be analyzed with simple-to-use tools, i.e., with a minimal amount of coding or training required, means domain experts can explore data sources alongside data experts. Many business intelligence tools have been developed to be simpler to use without reducing the quality of the output that can be created.

Even with domain expertise, analysts should be involved in forming the analytical outputs rather than just leaving everything to the SMEs. Analysts will have the experience to ask the right questions about the data to make sure as much value can be extracted from it as possible. If you are developing an analytical culture for the first time, there are some basic places to start developing analytical outputs. Asking about the who, what, when, where, and why of the categorical fields in the data set will help direct the analysis. Here is how you can use each of those aspects to explore a data source to foster a strong analytical output:

Who?
> This can look at internal individuals as well as customers and clients. Finding the individuals with the most records of data about them can indicate where your analysis should focus. Pareto's 80/20 principle (*https://oreil.ly/3-txt*) applies well in this circumstance where it is assumed that 80% of the benefit comes from 20% of the customers.

What?
> This angle of analysis can look at the products, services, or subjects covered by the data. Looking at new options versus the existing mainstays of an organization's suite of products is one of many angles that can be explored.

When?
> If you have any temporal data fields, you can look at how measures change over time. With any project delivery, understanding the effect of the project requires factoring in time.

Where?
> More business intelligence tools now offer the ability to map longitudes and latitudes when they are in a data source. Alternatively, some tools offer internal databases to map place names to longitudes and latitudes or geographical outlines of areas when they don't exist within the data source itself.

Why?
> This is the hardest of these questions to answer. The phrase "correlation does not equal causation" is common in analyst parlance for a reason.[1] A complete explanation of the causes of certain events covered in a data set is rarely fully captured by just its data fields. This is where domain expertise and experience help to position the data. Using data to support or challenge assumptions made by domain experts is the closest most analysts will get to really understanding the "why" through data.

Although business intelligence tools offer accessible ways for many people in an organization to produce their own analyses and contribute to forming an understanding of a situation, there are other methods available to support strong analyses. Code-centric solutions are growing in popularity. However, whether it is using R and Python

---

1 If you haven't explored this concept before, Tyler Vigen's "Spurious Correlations" infographic (*https://oreil.ly/H_h5X*) is a lighthearted demonstration of why correlation doesn't mean causation.

packages or BI tools that require some coding to use, the level of coding literacy needed limits who can use these solutions.

The benefit of tools that involve coding is that they provide a greater level of control and the possibility of bespoke solutions to deliver against the requirements. This can result in an increased sophistication as to how data is visualized, the use of data science models, or cheaper software costs compared to enterprise-ready business intelligence tools.

If your data projects deliver data products that involve AI or machine learning components, then it is very likely that you will be more reliant on central IT resources than on self-service reporting solutions that can be run out of individual domains in your organization.

Sharing with Others

When you have finished producing outputs from your project, you will have one final consideration: who can use them. The audience, or users of the data products, will dictate what you can create as well as the maintenance effort and likely level of follow-up work that is required.

You should have your audience in mind throughout the scoping and build process. Without this, it is unlikely you will create what it is that the end users actually need. Next, we'll discuss the key considerations for data products that will be used within your organization or externally by private organizations or shared publicly with anyone.

SHARING INTERNALLY WITH DEPARTMENTS

Sharing data products within your organization is often the primary aim of data projects. Developing data sources, producing reports, or making predictions for your own team or others usually means that you don't have to put too many restrictions on how the products are used.

After creating a data product, the more you can encourage the intended end users to use the product, the greater benefit you can potentially create. As I've previously noted, not everyone has high levels of data fluency; therefore, they may need support to effectively utilize the products. There are various types of support you can employ to ensure the product is used as intended:

Written explanations
> Providing step-by-step instructions on how to use your product is important to guide the end user. PDF guides or web pages on your intranet can be used to offer text descriptions along with screenshots of key parts of the process. These documents can be cheap to produce and are easy to distribute. PDFs are easily resharable, so care must be taken if there is any sensitive data in the screenshots you use.

Video walkthroughs

Although they are more costly and time-consuming to produce, videos can be a lot more descriptive as to how to use a product. Unless the video is very short, video files can be too large to share via email, so they need to be hosted somewhere. If the product contains sensitive information, the videos also need to be held in a secure location.

Training

The most expensive option can also have the biggest impact. Running training sessions on how to use a product can help guide users through generic use cases, but they will also help them use the product according to their preferences. It can be difficult to schedule training sessions due to the challenges of getting everyone together at the same time, whether in person or online. You will also need to ensure the trainer is sufficiently informed to be able to handle questions.

The wider the distribution of the data product, the more likely it is that support material will be required to ensure they use the product as intended. If a data product is for your own team, it's easier to persuade your team to use it. Once a product is shared with others, you need to be able to motivate them to use the product as well. Being clear on the product's benefits is challenging when there is so much competition for people's attention in a modern organization. Encouraging leaders to share the benefits of a product or ask questions that require usage of the product means it is more likely to get picked up.

Sometimes you will need to restrict other teams' and individuals' access to the project's output. There are a number of situations where you will need to restrict access; here are two important considerations to keep in mind:

Subject matter

Human resources (HR) teams have access to a lot of sensitive information and therefore must protect their data sources closely. Levels of pay, relationship statuses, and performance records are all sensitive information that needs to have restricted access. In addition, at publicly traded companies, finance teams will often have access to sensitive data. This information needs to be restricted to prevent insider trading and other illegal market practices.

Regulatory restrictions

Different industries face differing regulatory restrictions. For example, investment banks are restricted as to what data they can receive from their retail banking arm to prevent trades being undertaken based on restricted information, like the spending patterns of the bank's customers. In Europe, the ring fencing between investment and retail banks is also designed to limit the effects of poor trades. These restrictions extend to what data platforms can be shared between the divisions of the organization and hence the data products hosted on those platforms.

Many data and analytics platforms allow for restricted access based on logins so access can be controlled. Determining who should have access to your project's products is a key decision. Restrictions can be placed on the analytical outputs or on the underlying data source. If the analytical products have been carefully built to not expose sensitive information, then care must be taken to not expose details that may still exist in the underlying data set.

SHARING EXTERNALLY WITH PARTNERS

Sharing data with external parties can yield great benefits. The potential fiscal value increases dramatically when data is shared externally, as not only can your company benefit from selling the data products, but commercial partnerships can also be strengthened and shared propositions created.

The primary challenge with sharing data products externally is truly understanding what is required. If the external party is developing the end product for themselves, it's unlikely they will disclose exactly what they are trying to achieve. If the relationship isn't very strong between your organizations, they may fear you'll try to take the output to market first. This can make it difficult to produce the perfect product focused on their needs.

This won't be the case if the end product is a shared proposition. The challenge then becomes how you innovate together to form the concept in the first place. Certainly, through my (Carl's) career, potential partnerships between my organization and others were explored on the basis of delivering a shared proposition when we knew data sets likely existed. This makes creating the right data product for the end solution a longer process; in fact, it becomes another project in its own right.

All considerations you make when sharing your data products internally are made much harder when sharing your data products beyond your organization. You will need to think through many "What if?" scenarios to ensure you share the right information with the right people. If you get this part wrong, there can be serious consequences for allowing the misuse of data, even if you intended to do the right thing. Fines, reputational damage, and job loss could be the result if you frivolously neglect your duties of care with individuals' and your organization's data.

To avoid any of these negative consequences, you need to ensure you have the rights to allow your data to leave the organization. You'll regularly be asked to sign lengthy terms and conditions agreements that define how your data can be used and shared. If you plan to share your data products with third parties, you'll need to trace back the permissions in documents to ensure this is possible. You may have legal teams to support this type of work, but it still needs to be done carefully.

If your data products are shared with external parties, you need to ensure that you aren't sharing too much. You will need to check the data or outputs for commercially sensitive information about your organization. This may involve explicit insights shared in a visualized output or information hidden within the data set that forms the product.

Despite these challenges, the benefits of sharing data externally are huge. It is a revenue stream that is not leveraged anywhere near enough by most organizations. Sharing with other organizations opens up much larger opportunities and value than that derived from keeping the data internal—but even larger opportunities arise when sharing with the public.

SHARING EXTERNALLY WITH THE PUBLIC

Sharing data products with the public can provide a massive opportunity for a number of reasons:

Revenue opportunity
Charging a subscription model to allow people to see insights about their usage of a product or service has become a frequent model utilized by *quantified self applications* (*https://oreil.ly/lH6Ko*), like Strava, the fitness activity app.

Reason to use a product
Beeline, a cycling navigation device mentioned in the first chapter, provided data insights to its users to encourage more usage. Tracking speed, distance, and elevation traveled helps encourage users to keep using the Beeline device and application. Additionally, with sufficient anonymization, other users can be identified for the data, such as, in this case, city planners or store owners.

Making your customers smarter
A bank should become more affluent as their customers do due to their increased assets. By creating the ability for customers to learn about their spending habits through data insights, they may be able to find opportunities to save money.

When opening data products to the public, you need to be even more careful with what data is being shared and at what level of granularity. The largest downside of sharing data with the public is that you can lose their trust due to oversharing what information you are able to form from the use of your services. Assuring subjects that you are using their data carefully and privately should be at the heart of any data product shared with the public. If you break people's trust over how they expect you to use their data, you will find your organization receiving complaints and adverse media coverage, and potentially losing customers.

If you find value for the public use of your data products, the next challenge you will encounter is getting the public to use that product. Fighting for people's attention in a busy world is not easy. Due to the time you've spent developing the product, you are much more likely to perceive the value in your product than all of the potential users that the product could help. To grab people's attention, you might be tempted to use eye-catching charts and graphs, yet this might have an effect opposite to what you'd intend for the product's usage. Yet, by using more bespoke and potentially less decipherable charts, it is less likely that your audience will be able to interpret what you are sharing with them. Data fluency is a challenge, not just within organizations but throughout society. You may need to simplify charts and front-end design to make the product more accessible.

If you share a product with the public, it doesn't have to be aimed at the mass market. The contents of the data might naturally focus on benefits available to a small group of people, but when making the data publicly available, you still need to remove a lot of the complexity to allow those users to benefit from it.

Summary

Data projects can have many different inputs, leading to an infinite number of potential outputs. This means that no two data projects are going to be alike, which creates inherent management difficulties. From the outset, identifying the best data sources, acquiring the data, and bringing it into your organization will present challenges. Once you have the data, setting up the right storage setup, establishing cataloging, and producing the data products are all formidable tasks, but get it right and you can unlock a lot of value for your organization. The final consideration is who you are going to share the product of the project with.

Although data projects are technically challenging, delivering them effectively has become essential to any successful organization.

Building Your Analytics Platform

Whether you aim to build a simple dashboard highlighting basic company KPIs or a real-time predictive model to recommend products to customers, you will want to work backwards from the output to define the data architecture, design, tools, and people you will need to leverage to achieve this. This chapter will start with an overview of the current landscape of tools, data needs, and associated costs. It will end with some best practices, including Agile project management and building with quality and stakeholder trust in mind.

Technological Options

The AI hype has gone through several cycles of boom and bust. However, since 2010, we have seen an aggressive and steady push to inject more analytics and data savviness into nearly all industries and companies. To remain relevant and competitive, leaders have been pressured to learn and incorporate data and data systems into business decisions and product development pipelines. While some companies have lagged behind due to a lack of infrastructure or data expertise, or resistance to change, most companies have begun to leverage data to *inform* business decisions, and others have fully leaned in to create data-*driven* products. The industry, company, product, and leadership all impact the stage of data adoption and maturity they are and in what ways data is being leveraged.

In Chapter 1, we introduced the concept of *data-informed* decision-making. Applying this concept to companies, this implies a company that is leveraging data inputs to help support or guide the decision-making process but ultimately using human judgment to land on final decisions or strategy. This can be seen through the use of data to inform inventory management, pricing strategies, marketing, and product improvement. This behavior is common among more traditional companies (e.g., finance, healthcare, entertainment, and retail) that have historically relied heavily on human experience to guide decision-making processes. As data integration has become increasingly important to gain or keep a competitive edge, these companies have worked to lean in to incorporate more data-led decision-making. Data-informed decisions rely heavily on historical views, descriptive statistics, and dashboards for KPI monitoring, but predictive analytics can be leveraged and aid in decision-making as well.

When applicable, a company may develop *data-driven* decision-making through products that leverage data as the primary input to decision-making. Examples of this exist in nearly every application or technology we interact with nowadays, from personalized "for you" experiences from Netflix, Spotify, and YouTube to recommended routes and predicted drive time from Google Maps, Waze, and Apple Maps, and self-driving capabilities from Tesla. The list seems endless to encapsulate our reliance on products and services that are built on the back of big data and automated ML systems that drive real-time predictions. These companies have done a great job of building systems that continually position data at the center of their product development processes. However, even in what might seem like a hands-off system of inputs and outputs, there is always a need for human oversight. As seen with products like ChatGPT and Facebook, there are safety and quality assurance angles that will always require a level of human monitoring.

A company can have both data-driven and data-informed decision-making aspects. A company like Netflix is *data-driven* when forming personalized experiences on their app and is *data-informed* when making decisions within their finance and HR departments. Since some companies embody both decision-making types, this expands the collection of data products they use and the sophistication of the tools, storage solutions, and processes they will need to develop.

It all starts with an idea! A product, a service, or a gap in the existing marketplace is identified. Once leaders commit to *what* they will build, they then move on to *how*. How will it get built? How will success be measured? At the start of any company's formation, whether it was 100 years ago or a year ago, a myriad of key business decisions have been made to get the company up and running. As leaders then rush to build and prove relevance, the time to be thoughtful about analytics platform infrastructure is shortened, typically focused on short-term needs, and relies on existing expertise. Organizations will typically work to build a proof of concept on fragile infrastructure until value is shown. This leaves a lot of room for improvement, and typically companies evolve their perspectives and toolsets as they go through the different maturity stages that determine how easily they can pivot and adapt to changes in the technology landscape.

No matter what stage in this process you are currently in, whether it's rushing through the early establishment decision-making process or thoughtfully thinking through new technology systems to help support the next stage and evolution of your company, this chapter will provide you with the right tools and considerations to start off on the right foot. This will involve making decisions around analytic tools, data storage, and data process and pipelines.

ANALYTIC TOOLS

Your approach to data products will impact what your tech stack looks like (i.e., the tools you've decided to rely on for the data outputs you will be producing). Based on the data products you aim to establish within your organization (basic analytics, dashboards, forward-looking views, etc.), you will be faced with many tool options that have different data requirements and needs. The specific tools you choose will depend on the type of data you have, the questions you want to answer, and your technical skills and resources. Let's take a look at the major tool types, while highlighting some options you can consider for each:

Spreadsheet software

The first and most common software that drives nearly all businesses in some fashion are spreadsheets. This software is powerful and can be used to store, analyze, visualize, and even predict data. Excel (Microsoft) and Google Sheets (G-suite) tend to dominate this space, and their usage numbers only continue to grow. The latest statistic on usage put Excel reliance by companies at about 63 percent.[1] When it comes to quick and accessible data analysis, nothing tops spreadsheets.

Typically, spreadsheets are used as an early solution for individuals and smaller teams. In my (Sarah's) experience, I've even seen some larger companies relying on spreadsheets as the main data storage system as well! This becomes limiting once the data becomes too large and more sophisticated analytics are being requested. Still, much of the operational and ad hoc reporting covered in Chapter 2 can be handled with spreadsheet software.

Low-code/no-code data analytics

When your data volume or complexity grows, running repetitive data preparation, cleaning, and reporting tasks can become very time consuming, and you might want to turn to other software options. Low-code or no-code data analytics platforms like KNIME, RapidMiner, and Alteryx all offer drag-and-drop interfaces to help build data preparation workflows, analytics, and dashboarding. Each tool will provide a different set of features, and you'll want to explore each to land on the one that works best for your needs.

---

1 StackCommerce, "63 Per Cent of Companies Consider Excel a Vital Accounting Tool," *Financial Post*, April 29, 2021, *https://oreil.ly/1a37R*.

Shifting your data prep, analysis, and visualization over to one of these tools will help you "work smarter, not harder" by streamlining your processes and empowering non-technical users to perform more sophisticated analysis. In addition to helping automate processes, added features of these tools include the ability to collaborate with your peers, version control, and data quality monitoring. Spreadsheets can be prone to human error and lack the necessary controls for data governance. These tools help circumvent those concerns.

BI software

The next group of tools are business intelligence tools like Tableau, Looker, Power BI, Qlik, or Incorta that can be used to visualize and analyze data in near real time, create interactive dashboards, and generate reports for decision-making. Features across these tools will vary, but many of them incorporate low-code or no-code interfaces, with drag-and-drop and pre-built components, making them accessible to users without extensive programming knowledge. Additionally, this software provides rich collaboration, sharing, and distribution options.

One major drawback to BI tools like this is that the ETL process required to get data ready to visualize will typically involve data pipelines built outside of these tools. Some tools, like Tableau, have developed prep tools like Tableau Prep that allow power users (*https://oreil.ly/t4Zkb*) to own their pipeline workflows in a similar and familiar tool. However, when prep tools like this are not available, data engineering resources may be needed to help build the workflows and provide data tables for your use cases.

Statistical/machine learning (ML) software

For large and complex data sets or if you need more flexibility and customization beyond what traditional BI tools may provide, advanced statistical software like Python, R, or SAS can be leveraged. Libraries for visualization like Matplotlib, seaborn, and ggplot can be used to produce publication-quality graphs and charts, and libraries for machine learning like scikit-learn or Carat can be used to develop predictive models, classify data, or automate decision-making processes.

Python and R have grown in popularity due to the availability of powerful libraries, the myriad of software established to help manage, test, create, develop, and deploy ML solutions, and their open source nature. *Open source* refers to a software's open and generally free nature, where the source code is made publicly available and generally anyone is free to use it without paying for a license. In addition to being free to use, the tools are improved through crowdsourcing, which means anybody can contribute to adding new features, fixing bugs, and optimizing performance.

Adopting statistical and machine learning software has a few barriers to entry, including learning a programming language, understanding statistical concepts, and familiarity with setting up development environments. With open source software, the barrier might be a little lower due to all the resources made available by the community, but still take time and effort to learn. Luckily, AutoML (*https://oreil.ly/6uRH-*) tools abstract away much of the complexity of machine learning, making it easier for non-experts to build and deploy models.

Depending on your needs, you may find yourself using one or many of the tools just presented. Most organizations, regardless of size, will have some reliance on spreadsheets and BI tools as a way of sharing data across the company. If you end up leveraging statistical or ML software, you'll likely find yourself piping the output into a spreadsheet or BI tool for wider consumption by the company. Although reading from a code-heavy Jupyter Notebook may work for some folks, it won't work for a wider audience.

Especially in large companies with established processes and numerous people working on similar goals, there may be an over-reliance on the limited features of spreadsheets in data-informed parts of the business. However, we are slowly starting to see more technical skills trickling into those areas, which could improve process and output. This is largely in part to the democratization of data and tools within organizations and a general emphasis on data literacy. This process involves simplifying and broadening the means to access and analyze data.

As you look to rationalize your existing analytical stack, it's important to continue to watch the landscape as it continues to change and evolve. We are seeing this with continued integrations of technology tools, such as Google Sheets integrating with Big-Query and ChatGPT and books teaching Python for Excel (*https://oreil.ly/93GhQ*).

DATA STORAGE AND MANAGEMENT

As you continue to focus on your data product and the inputs needed for the desired output, you will need to ask *how much* data you will need and *where* to store it.

Live snapshots are needed for real-time reporting and monitoring of week over week (WoW) and day over day (DoD) changes and help answer questions like these: How has revenue changed WoW or DoD? What was our biggest customer yesterday? Which product drove the highest revenue last week? Real-time reporting is great for things like assessing business health or giving a quick view of KPIs in an easy to read and understand format (typically a well-formatted spreadsheet or dashboard). This allows the business to react appropriately to any unexpected behavior in KPIs (good or bad).

The word *live* gives you the impression that the data is updated by the second (or even more frequently), but more realistically, there are lags between when the data was created, where it was stored, and the data pipelines built to get it to you. Depending on the setup of your existing ETL process and the complexity of the pipeline, this may be a delay of an hour or a day, or even longer. Either way, you might consider the latest view possible to be "live."

Historical tables extend time horizons (or time frames) back to a year and beyond, allowing us to compare longer-term trends—things like evaluating year over year (YoY) and seasonal trends or driving predictive modeling. Changes in metrics today could be explained by a "normal" fluctuation, but you'd need the historical data to suss that out. Depending on how familiar you are with the metrics, KPIs, and the culture of your team or company, you will likely see a lot of reactionary behavior.

An example of this is advertiser spending during Ramadan, shown in Figure 4-1. In the Middle East and North Africa (MENA), advertisers will spend up on food delivery services in preparation for Eid. This will mean elevated levels of spending leading up to and during the month of Ramadan. However, the end of Eid signifies the end of Ramadan spending, and you will typically see a large revenue drop-off (similar to the cliff you see after New Year's in Western and Chinese cultures). Understanding relevant regional behavior and having historical data to set and confirm expectations, and even predict the current year's drop-off, can be helpful ways of guiding the business and can help it move from a reactive "fire drill" mindset to a more proactive "how do we offset the dip" one.

Thus, we come back to the question of "how much data to store and where?" The answer will depend on the needs and the cost. Data storage options and costs have evolved over the years, from floppy disks to cloud storage that allows for more data to be stored more reliably and more cost-effectively. This has enabled the volume and variety of data we can store to broaden and incorporate more use cases and business needs, and this sometimes leads to a "let's track this for now and see if we need it later" mentality. As a result, it's become common to have more data than is necessary to accommodate the needs of the business. However, even if that may be a sound approach, it's important to understand the needs of all of the stakeholders before making a final decision on what data should live where and, at what storage level, to ensure that none of the "must-haves" is missed. Understanding which metrics are needed, by which teams, and in what historical time horizon, is important to make the right storage decisions. Teams predicting future revenue will need multiple years of revenue to identify and understand trends, seasonal patterns, holiday dependence, etc. Without easy access to historical data, the finance and revenue strategy teams are limited in their forecasting abilities.

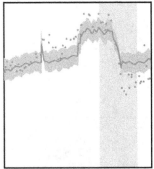

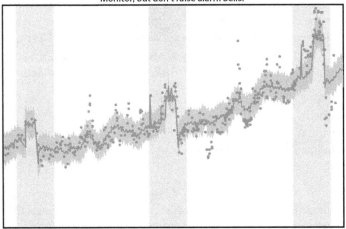

Figure 4-1. Short versus longer time horizons

There are three major types of storage that you may consider when balancing the trade-off between cost and accessibility: hot, warm, and cold (see Figure 4-2). After doing some due diligence and gathering requirements, you can then make choices around which data to store and at what level.

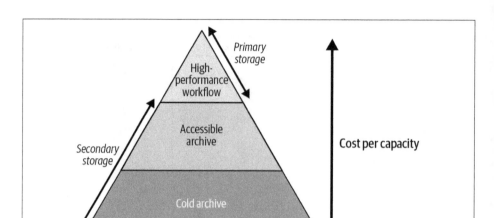

Figure 4-2. Storage pyramid (adapted from an image by Anne Herreria (https://oreil.ly/21jj-))

Hot storage
> To manage the demands of near-real-time reporting and live snapshots of data, you will need that data living in what's called hot storage. This type of storage option is meant to store data that is accessed frequently, and it offers the highest level of performance. This is also typically more expensive than other storage options.

Warm storage
> For data that is needed less frequently, warm storage is the next possible option that can handle data that needs to be readily available. This type of storage is less expensive than hot storage, but still offers relatively fast access times.

Cold storage
> Cold storage is designed for data that is rarely accessed but needs to be stored for long periods of time. This type of storage is the least expensive, but offers the slowest access times. This could be data that is archived for compliance reasons.

DATA PROCESSES AND PIPELINES

To get the output you desire, you'll need to ensure that the inputs are available *how* you need them, *when* you need them, and at the *rate* at which you need them.

If you're working through an *ad hoc* (or one-off) analysis, you are typically OK working with snapshots of data provided to you by the source owner. If you don't have ready access to certain types of data or data sets, you can typically request and work off of one-off data pulls that can help satisfy the need.

Additionally, ad hoc data pulls can be very helpful in building out *proof of concept*. When you are working to establish value from a new analysis, approach, or process, it's likely that the data inputs you require don't exist in a scaled format yet. Leveraging data snapshots is a great way to take a first pass, get feedback from stakeholders, iterate, and perfect the output. Building a proof of concept is an important part of the cycle of building data products at scale and can be used to position arguments for why to invest in a third-party vendor or in building internal pipelines for your use case. This will move your one-off task into a *continuous* need, and you'll be presented with a few options of how to proceed from there.

If your team has dedicated BI or engineering support, you can work closely with them to get an end-to-end process to support the use case. Alternatively, you can leverage one of the many self-service tools mentioned in "Analytic Tools" on page 89 to help automate the workflows yourself. In the absence of IT support or investment in self-serve data analytics tools, your team members may find other ways to build their pipelines, such as leveraging open source tools like Python, R, cron jobs, etc. In these situations, you may find scrappy team members building their own pipelines. Generally, building in isolation can have its pros and cons. On one hand, this provides the team a way to build out new processes quickly and without dependence on other teams. However, this can be problematic when the skills on the team are limited and can't be extended to support production-style code and structure, and will need consistent oversight to ensure stability. This means the process will continue to live in a sub-optimal state.

Those companies that have optimally set up their teams with the tools or team structure to support the right data needs will have one additional layer of process that will help them run effectively: data governance. *Data governance* encompasses all the practices, processes, policies, and guidelines across the company that ensure data quality, integrity, and availability.

Once you've proved value from your data product, you will need to invest in time and resources to build out scaled and production-level backend data pipelines to ensure you are able to support the data product you've created on a *continuous* basis. You'll need to establish things like the dimensions and measures you need, the level of granularity required, and the frequency at which data is to be refreshed.

How to Choose an Analytical Architecture

Landing on your analytical architecture can be challenging as you manage budget constraints, the skill makeup of your team, differing leadership styles, and the reality of how long it takes to make or create change within a team or organization. In this section, we will dive into the considerations factoring into these decisions.

ASSESSING TOTAL COST OF OWNERSHIP

They say "nothing in life is free," and this applies to your data product (or suite of data products) as well! To bring your vision to life, you'll need a combination of people, tools, and processes. Each component has an associated cost that you'll need to take into consideration as a part of the *total cost of ownership* (TCO). The TCO represents the cost associated with the product throughout its lifetime, from deployment to deprecation, and everything in between. In a world with many open source tools to leverage, making use of them can help with some of the cost, but there are still many other factors to consider:

People

> The first consideration is people. Do you have the right skills on the team to accomplish and build what you've set out to produce? You'll need to keep in mind analytics skills, modeling skills, engineering abilities, creativity, product management, etc. This cost will include salaries, for data scientists, data engineers, business analysts, and any other team members involved. In some cases, you will need to hire a consultancy or bring on partners to help evaluate and determine the best execution plan. Additional costs include employee benefits, recruitment costs, the cost of training team members on new tools and technologies, and ongoing training to keep their skills up to date.

Tools

> The second consideration involves data, tools, and technology. Let's talk about the data first—this includes the cost of acquiring and storing data, as well as any fees associated with using third-party data sources. Getting refined with exactly what data you need, and in what time horizons, can help bring down your total cost here. This includes third-party data and the needs and costs associated with enriching your first-party data. Third-party data and licenses can be very expensive, so think carefully about what subset of the data is necessary to meet the needs of your outlined use cases. Can you combine use cases across the company? Can you get ahead of all the needs and create a centralized source for this? As time goes on, the volume of data will continue to increase, so you'll want to continue to re-evaluate the scope of the needs and adjust data storage options accordingly. What can be moved from hot to warm or warm to cold storage?

> Next, you'll need to think about the tools or technology needed, which can include expenses for licenses for analytical software tools, data governance tools, and any hardware or cloud services. These tool costs will vary and may need to be calculated based on the number of users (e.g., Tableau) or total usage (e.g., Amazon Redshift). Do you have the right tools in place to accomplish what you've set out to do? Again, many companies will "run" with a default choice that you'll need to evaluate as a part of this process. Does it work for your needs? Does your team need a different tool? If so, what's the cost of the tool, and how does it compare to the existing contract?

Sometimes you might decide that an existing tool is no longer sufficient, and migration to another tool is needed. In general, migrations can be incredibly lengthy processes, as teams take time to process the changes, go through training to understand the new tool, build in time to migrate, and then work to rebuild processes and reports into the new tool. It usually follows the cycle of grief, as your engineers and analysts go from denial to anger to bargaining, and finally to acceptance. Additionally, it can involve the cost of changing contracts, which in and of itself can land you with much higher costs than the original contract. Existing contracts are often years old and can have the advantage of legacy pricing, making them very hard to beat.

If there is no migration process or you've completed the migration, then comes the cost of maintaining and updating the technology and tools you are using, as well as any ongoing support costs.

Processes

The last consideration is the cost of processes, as there are implied costs to your resources when bad processes are being followed. Taking the time to evaluate how processes may be broken and can be improved can likely increase the value of the output of any limited resources you may have. A process improvement can include training your team on how to write more cost-efficient code and developing code review processes. Another example could be encouraging more close collaboration across teams and developing communication and knowledge sharing forums to improve output. It could also mean establishing roles and responsibilities around how teams engage with one another on projects or data workflows. The list is endless, but I hope this gives you an idea of how you can use process improvements to lower your overall costs.

SPEED OF BUSINESS CHANGE

At this point, you've successfully evaluated the tools, the cost, and the general scope of needs for your data product, and you may start to ask...what comes next? Well, the unfortunate truth is that the journey only gets harder from here, so get prepared! It's time to put the technology aside and see how well you can lean on your relationships and connect with and incentivize people to change. The first step will require buy-in from leadership teams and executives, which will be critical to any successful data project. You'll want to be ready to answer questions like: why the change? And why now?

Your answers should consider the lens of your audience. Are they leaders who are less familiar with data technologies and may be less able to understand the implications of the changes being made or may be more resistant to change in general? Conversely, are they more data-savvy leaders who may be more likely to embrace new technologies and approaches but may also have higher expectations for the benefits that these changes will deliver? Either way, you'll want to prepare the right pitch for your product, your proposal, and *yourself*. Remember that big investments are not just given to good ideas, they're given to great leaders, so don't forget about the importance of your role in bringing this to life.

You'll likely end up in weeks, months, and sometimes even years of debate, as it takes time to gain consensus among leaders, approve budgets, allocate resources, and move into the execution phase. The time it will take to move through this phase will in large part depend on the scope of change requested and the data culture of the organization or team. Are you asking for additional head count? Ingestion of new data sources? A platform shift? Migration to the cloud? Major rebuilds of data pipelines and data stores? Not all leaders are fully leaned in to the data opportunity and will need more time and repetition to get them fully on board, and even those who are fully leaned in may not have the budget at the time of your request to get things approved. Be patient with this part of the process, but also don't get discouraged and give up!

Now, let's assume you've made it to the other side of the approval process and want to move into execution—let's talk brass tacks on what it will take to follow through till the end of what you've promised. Many factors will impact how quickly you can move, including the size of your organization, the complexity of the existing data infrastructure, the scope of the changes being made, and the level of technical expertise of the leaders and employees involved. There are some major factors to keep in mind:

Size of the team

> The first consideration that will impact the speed of change is the size of the company (or team). In smaller teams, changing data architecture may be less complex but still require significant effort and present unique challenges. Smaller organizations may have less technical expertise in-house and face resource constraints, such as limited budgets or a lack of dedicated IT staff. This can make it difficult to plan and execute changes effectively. Your challenge here will be finding a means to be effective with limited resources. Sometimes this can mean leaning on consultants where possible; other times you'll need to move more slowly, and another option you might consider is deprioritizing team members' projects to focus on the migration.

> In larger businesses with more complex data infrastructures, there may be multiple legacy systems that need to be integrated or migrated, and the process of mapping data flows between these systems can be time consuming and prone to error. Efforts to migrate will involve a high level of coordination, likely across many people and multiple teams. As you work through this process, you may find a need to hire new personnel with specialized technical skills to manage the new architecture, which will add to the time requirements and complexity of the

process. At times, transitioning the team will feel like redirecting a cruise ship through turbulent waters, and you have to be ready to steer.

Scope and complexity

There are various levels of change that can be introduced into a team, which include (but are not limited to) storage migration, application migration, business process migration, and data migration. Whether one or more of these changes are being proposed, you'll want to think through the complexity of the existing infrastructure. Have you carefully analyzed and understood the existing data systems, including their structure, content, and dependencies? Typically, the longer the reliance on a set of tools or infrastructure, the higher the complexity and the more time you will need to spend carefully planning to manage potential points of failure or data losses. After the migration, you'll need to set aside time for validation and potential decommissioning of old processes or tools. The scope of your changes should be well thought out and outlined, with a timeline including any changes and expectations you have of the teams you'll be anticipating to move from one system to another.

Business leadership

Above and beyond the initial sign-off for you to start building, you will need leadership support all the way through the migration and adoption phases. You will likely run into challenges and roadblocks along the way and will need leadership on your side to help unblock them, so be sure to ask for this up front. Alignment and communication from leadership will help make your life easier as you start enforcing migration deadlines.

Overall, the challenges involved in migrating and changing analytical architecture can be significant and require careful planning, execution, and ongoing management to ensure a successful transition. Don't forget that underlying all this change are humans, and research shows that habit formation and breaking can take anywhere between 18 and 254 days.[2] So remember to keep your empathy muscle strong and stay in close communication with all teams that will be impacted by the changes to ensure things move smoothly and successfully. Overcommunication can help bring people along on this journey with you by providing context around purpose-setting (why are we doing this) and timelines (when are we doing this).

---

2 Suzy Davenport, "How Long Does It Take to Break a Habit and What Is the Best Way to Do It?" *Medical News Today*, October 11, 2022, *https://oreil.ly/5C4aC*.

HOW WILL IT BE USED?

Before the implementation phase starts, you'll have to make a decision about how you will approach the migration: *big bang* or *trickle*. Big bang migrations involve moving all the data from an existing system to a new system in a single, large-scale operation. At small scales, this is a clean and effective approach. However, for larger, more complex systems, this could be risky, involving significant downtime and data loss or corruption if things go wrong. In theory, this approach should cost less than a trickle approach if all things go smoothly and risks are mitigated correctly.

Alternatively, you can move more slowly and take the trickle approach. This would involve moving data or processes in small, incremental stages, over a longer period of time. This approach can be less disruptive and less risky, as it provides more time to test and validate the new system before switching over. The main downside to a trickle approach is the challenge of maintaining two systems for an extended period of time to ensure proper transitions. This requires more people-power and will end up costing much more to maintain.

INTERNAL TEAM VERSUS EXTERNAL SUPPORT

The last consideration, but inherently also a part of each component, is *people*. *Who* will you be leaning on to bring your vision to life? Will it be the existing team members, or will you be looking to hire contract workers? You can help yourself arrive at the answer to this question by analyzing the trade-off between cost and time.

If you have time constraints, need to move quickly, and lack the required skills on the team, you'll want to consider bringing in temporary contractors or consultants to help move things along. The trade-off here is the cost, as consultants are expensive. Alternatively, you can work to up-level your existing team through investment in learning and development training. This process will take much longer and will involve a different type of cost—the cost of potential mistakes that can be made in the process of learning. The people aspect of each project is nuanced, and we will discuss this in more detail in Chapter 5.

Deployment

The deployment phase will be where you start building and your vision will come to life as tangible output for your end users. This can be the most exciting part, since the impact of your work can start to be really felt at this stage. If you're ready, there are a few things to keep in mind; let's walk through them together.

AGILE DEVELOPMENT

The gold standard for project management used to be the *waterfall method*, which involved extensive effort to gather up-front requirements (aka *specs*), months of building in isolation, little to no modifications to those original specs, and the release to stakeholders only once the product was fully built. This meant that no feedback was provided until the product was fully completed, leaving little room for flexibility and iteration. At this point, stakeholders might have gotten smarter about what they wanted and often had extensive feedback on the product once it was delivered. Fortunately, just as technology is changing, methodologies and processes around it are changing as well. This is where *Agile* comes in.

This may not be the first time you hear about Agile methodology, but what is it exactly, and how will it help you? Well, Agile focuses on a flexible, iterative, and customer-centric approach. Before starting any project, you will go through a similar gathering of requirements from stakeholders, but the difference here is that you will use *MoSCoW* prioritization, which allows features and requests to get prioritized through a series of questioning that will help you land on the Must-haves, Should-haves, Could-haves, and Won't-haves. Through this process, you can start to simplify the expected output into a version made of only the must-haves, also known as *minimum viable product* (MVP). Starting with an MVP will help shorten the time it takes to build, get feedback, and iterate. Adapting an Agile approach to product development can be critical to setting up your output for success.

Let's say you work at a social media company and have been asked to build a benchmarking tool that helps identify industries that are accelerating their advertising spending. You have been asked to develop an output that joins multiple data sources together, both first and third party, and that provides an internal view as well as a full market view. To develop an MVP, you might suggest narrowing down to just first-party data and developing good internal benchmarks. This could satisfy the needs of stakeholders until you are able to layer in third-party data. Joining in third-party data would involve mapping the data sets, performing quality assurance to ensure accuracy, and validating impact based on the KPIs intended for the analysis. In most cases where third-party data is being used in a *descriptive* way, there is a clear path to add value, so this can be very well worth the time investment.

PLAN DEPLOYMENT

The first step of any good deployment plan is understanding all the downstream impacts resulting from the changes you are making. You will have done most of this during the scoping phase, when you reached out to the relevant teams, but it's always good to maintain a strong communication flow with your end users, as requirements may change over time. Once this is done, be sure to share the timeline, milestones, contingency plans, and communication protocols with them so they know what to expect and when. Make sure all teams (IT, data engineering, business intelligence, data science, analysis, or other teams) are looped in and understand their role in the process. To that end, ensure the communication protocols and expectations are clear. Communicating early and often and using multiple formats (email, Slack, one-on-ones) will help mitigate issues down the line, so spend time ensuring you are sending clear, concise, and frequent updates to all relevant team members.

Once you've moved into deployment, you'll want to verify that everything is working as intended by testing, monitoring, and evaluating changes in a controlled environment. Thus, deployment will typically have two stages that you'll want to accommodate for: testing and production. Let's cover what happens in both:

Testing

The testing phase is an important part of deployment, as it will help minimize the risk of errors or disruptions. Start with an MVP and take your time in this phase, ensuring your end users are involved. This will alert you early on as to whether you are satisfying their needs or not and allow them time to give feedback. During the testing phase, you'll have time to evaluate and course-correct, which will be hard to do once you've productionalized and rolled out the changes. You will need to be ready for anything, such as changes in scope, incompatibility issues, data loss, etc., and you may realize that you need to pivot to accommodate unforeseen issues. Make adjustments as necessary, and continue to gather feedback from team members to identify areas for improvement. One of my (Sarah's) favorite quotes about following plans is from the fictional character Leonard Snart from the TV show *Arrow*:

> *"Doesn't matter. There are only four rules you need to remember: make the plan, execute the plan, expect the plan to go off the rails, throw away the plan. Follow my lead and you'll be fine."*

Production

As you move into the release phase, where you deploy the changes to a production environment, you'll want to ensure you update any related documentation and communicate the changes to end users. Take the lead to set up training, user guides, and other resources to help team members adapt to the changes.

To mitigate risk when moving through the development phase, you will want to lean on Agile risk management policies to help continually monitor and address issues. This involves a collaborative approach among the development team, project managers, and stakeholders to identify and prioritize risks and develop strategies to mitigate them.

USE ANALYSIS TECHNIQUES TO MONITOR DEPLOYMENT

After deployment is complete, you'll want to closely monitor, and aim to improve, your data pipelines and products' health, quality, and performance. This is known as *data observability*, and it's not a new concept. Traditionally, it was limited to monitoring individual components of a fairly simple data stack, and data quality checks were often performed manually. From a reporting standpoint, this might look like this: end users such as subject matter experts seeing breaks in reporting (a day of missing data, an outlier, or a weird data point), alerting business intelligence teams on the issue, and suggesting a break in the data pipeline or QA flow. This leveraged a *bottom-up* approach to data observability that relied on SMEs to drive quality checks on reporting. However, modern data observability practices include automated data quality checks, anomaly detection, and real-time monitoring of the data pipelines that live within the engineering and BI teams. This has led to a general shift towards a more *top-down*, proactive, and automated approach to monitoring, observing, and actioning improvements to meet SLA requirements and keep data quality high. Let's cover some of the important aspects of building strong data observability practices within your organization.

First, you'll want to define the metrics to monitor (number of sales, daily revenue, number of clicks, etc.) and establish acceptable ranges for these metrics such that when data points lie outside of "normal" ranges, you are able to develop automated alerts and notifications to observe or fix them. This is most often referred to as *outlier detection* and is an important component of the data observability framework. Making this more automated helps engineering and BI teams notice and resolve issues before they land in, or break, reporting.

Second, you'll want to monitor the health of data pipelines to ensure that data flows smoothly from its source to its destination. With many systems coming together to form data sets and reporting, there are many points of failure that can lead to delays or gaps in the data. This could be due to human error, hardware failures, software malfunctions, or numerous other reasons. For example, the data may be lost if an application crashes while writing data to a database. Thus, setting up mitigation plans to handle data latency and data loss issues will be critical for sustaining data integrity and meeting your agreed-on SLA requirements.

Third, you'll want to regularly review the alerts, notifications, and reports generated by data observation practices to identify trends and insights. When running high-level analytics on the reporting you've built to monitor your data systems, you will be able to uncover things like: Are there any patterns for when data fails? On weekends? On Monday mornings when everyone is competing for resources? What do usage metrics look like, and how often are end users leveraging reporting built for them a month ago or a year ago? Can we deprecate reports that are no longer being leveraged? And the list goes on...

Finally, you'll want to monitor the usage of any established reporting or data sets. This is the best way to know if what you've built is going to good use! Depending on the tools used, you may have some built-in analytics that will monitor usage.

Having strong data observability practices in place can help your team get ahead of data quality issues, establishing more transparency and allocating responsibility to them to ensure that reporting is accurate and reliable. Coming back to our theme of stakeholder trust, building strong data observability practices can help strengthen the trust between your team and your end users. Over time, this has only a positive ripple effect.[3]

Develop Through Use

Despite appearing as the last section of this chapter, developing through business use cases is where all good data products should start. Let's be honest—not all fun data projects are impactful, and not all impactful business problems are fun, but there is a large middle ground where much great work can be done. So, grounding your work on what can move the needle for your business is where your work should start.

CREATE KEY REPORTS/DASHBOARDS

The data savviness of your organization will help guide what you tackle first, how you aim to build trust, and how you'll show immediate value. Any newly established team, product, or output takes time to gain traction and achieve adoption. It is in this spirit that you should aim to develop products that have clear benefits. Take an audit of what currently exists, and look for areas to add value. If dashboards and key reports already exist, where are there areas of opportunity for either automation or optimization?

Automation

> Automation refers to the use of technology to perform tasks or move through processes that would otherwise be handled manually by individuals on the team. You can easily identify where your team is spending a lot of time on repetitive processes that can use some form of automation. Investment in automated solutions for frequent, repetitive tasks will help free up their bandwidth to do more with their time and help improve the accuracy of their output. If stakeholders are relying on output from these processes, this also has downstream implications that improve on your SLA delivery.

Optimization

> Optimization refers to the process of finding the best solution to a problem or task. It's very common for teams to adopt methodologies that stay somewhat consistent over time, allowing for very little creativity or improvements to be made. Humans are hard to change, and established processes are hard to alter. However, the introduction of new and different approaches not only can be helpful but can also improve the accuracy and quality of product output. We

---

3 For more on data observability, see *Fundamentals of Data Observability* or *What Is Data Observability?*, both authored by Andy Petrella and published by O'Reilly.

encourage you to look and question the modes of operation to find areas of opportunity to optimize for better processes and solutions. Get others involved and hear people's thoughts and ideas about the existing workflow. Are they itching to change it but just don't have time or the skills to do so?

Building Trust

At the heart of any data product(s) you create is ensuring you have the trust of stakeholders and executives in the company. Trust takes a long time to build, and you may be set up for success (with past data teams leaving a strong positive impression), or you may need to work to rebuild that trust. Personally, there have been teams I've (Sarah) joined where trust was so low that it was incredibly hard to garner adoption on the data output I was creating. It took many months, my persistence despite the headwinds, and the "output speaking for itself" to finally see the tides turn around. Eventually, stakeholders were relying so heavily on the output of the models I had created that it had become a crucial and necessary part of the decision-making process. This is only to say, don't give up if you feel push back initially! Understand that this is a long process that involves trust in people and trust in output. Thus, I would encourage you to start simple—take a small process and improve it slightly, and then move on to bigger and more complex projects. Also, involve your stakeholders early to give them a voice in the process and an idea of the changes they will be expecting. Seeing themselves as thought partners and contributors to the output can help build trust faster, and in turn, they'll champion the results.

QUALITY VERSUS QUANTITY

At the heart of any successful data product are high levels of adoption and trust. In the early days of Facebook, Mark Zuckerberg established the motto "move fast and break things." Although this was a great way to experiment, build fast, and attract attention for his product, it was not a sustainable framework to keep for the long term. In 2022, at the time of the rebrand to Meta, and due to some negative press around the callousness implied by moving quickly without regard, they shifted to "move fast with stable infrastructure." This example highlights the importance of moving quickly enough to prove value but also cautions against moving so quickly that many mistakes are made and trust is broken.[4]

Especially in the beginning, you'll need to consider the trade-off between building for speed and building for quality. On one extreme, you can move very quickly and risk losing trust with stakeholders if output is wrong or misleading. On the other extreme, you can move so slowly, requiring lengthy timelines to get things completed and shipped, that you can leave stakeholders wondering when the promised output will be delivered. The key is to land somewhere in the middle of this spectrum, moving quickly enough to deliver value but slowly enough to validate and ensure accurate output. A great place to start is with any low-hanging fruit that can deliver high value and can be achieved with little effort. As you watch your team or stakeholders receive, consume, and process information, watch the flow and output. How robust are the analytics, dashboarding, and real-time analytics? Can you start integrating predictive modeling into the stack? Find creative ways to provide automation or optimization to their workflows in an impactful and straightforward manner.

When delivering data products, it's important to remember that you are the owner of that product for the lifetime of its existence and use. The one exception here will be when there is an established process for handing over your work to engineering teams who will work to stabilize the output through productionalization. Once your product is out in the wild, your stakeholders may broaden; and in the absence of engineering support, you'll want to be prepared to handle questions around the output and fix the backend processes if anything breaks. Thus, you will need to monitor your output to ensure stakeholders continue to get, and see, the right output. Often, depending on who has built the backend pipelines and if it was built on fragile infrastructure, you will need to monitor this closely.

Consider this an ongoing iterative loop. Similar to Brian McKnight's lyrics, "if ever I believe my work is done, then I'll start back at one," you'll want to continue to look for opportunities to improve on infrastructure, data enrichment, tools, and processes. You may find yourself involved in multiple negotiations for more resources or better tools, and this will all start from working through the needs of your stakeholders.

---

4 Emily Stewart, "Mark Zuckerberg's New Values for Meta Show He Still Hasn't Truly Let Go of 'Move Fast and Break Things,'" *Business Insider*, February 2, 2022, *https://oreil.ly/8hQBc.*

Setting Your Team Up for Success

People are at the heart of all technology. Despite what may seem like a grim view of robots on the rise and technology systems taking over jobs, people are the center of all technology decisions and implementation. Putting the right talent in front of the right problems and investing in people to build for the future is where your leadership can be truly felt.

Recruiting

When Harvard Business Review (*https://oreil.ly/30Gpb*) dubbed "data scientist" the "sexiest job of the 21st century" in 2012, this raised awareness of the importance of data jobs (data analyst, data scientist, data engineer, data storyteller, etc.) when it comes to business outcomes. Although the true business impact was yet to be proved and the differences between data titles blurry, the race to hire and retain the best talent was on—and the competition was grueling! Tremendous pressure was put on companies to provide large compensation packages and offer outstanding benefits to attract candidates in their direction. Naturally, existing data-centric companies were ahead of the curve, with established data teams, already existing reliance on data systems, and they set the bar for data practice standards. It's no wonder that all the best talent was sitting at FANG (Facebook, Amazon, Netflix, and Google), among other large tech companies. They were offering large comp packages, but in exchange, they were asking for a candidate with exceptional technical, strategic, leadership, and domain expertise—an all-around unicorn.

But the pool of "unicorn" candidates was limited and shrinking by the day. To continue hiring at scale, these expectations had to be reset, and compromises and trade-offs needed to be made. Understanding that you may find a technically strong candidate who lacks domain experience or vice versa meant accepting that an investment in learning and development was not just beneficial, but necessary. In the case where you were not willing to settle for anything less than the perfect candidate, well, your only enemy would be time. How long could you wait before filling this role? How would projects and deliverables be impacted by keeping this role open for an extended period of time? Ultimately, your decision would need to factor in time to find the right candidate, cost to hire, and an investment in learning and development (L&D).

The limited number of unicorns in the market forced a shift towards unicorn data teams rather than individuals, wherein the team members complemented each other's skills (data science, domain knowledge, communication, operations). As you evaluate and audit your existing team and the skills you'll need to execute on your project vision, you may find there may be some gaps, and you'll be faced with the trade-off between upskilling the existing team and looking for new talent to fill the skills gap. Let's take a look at the elements to consider when making the decision to go either way.

INTERNAL FIRST

Of course, the best place to start building your vision is through your existing team! They are your all-stars who know the business intimately, they have the strongest domain expertise, and they can be your anchor to ensure the process moves smoothly. They understand the nuances of the data and the importance of key metrics, calculations, reports, pipelines, etc. So, take an audit of your existing talent. Do any of them possess the right skills to assist with the changes? If so, what projects would they need to pause in order to take on this project? Are these projects mission-critical or would the business understand if things were put on hold in order to prioritize your work? Your major decision here will be the trade-off between existing and new projects and ultimately deciding which one may have the bigger long-term impact on the business.

If specialists on your team do not already exist, do you have trainable talent (i.e., they are easily teachable and motivated)? If so, there are a couple questions worth evaluating here: Are the skills you aim to train additive to the long-term needs of the team? Are the skills additive to that person's career based on what direction they want to go? These questions will help you understand if an investment in learning and development could be worthwhile.

Once you've decided, team members will need to navigate through many options for learning, including but not limited to books, MOOCs (Massive Open Online Courses), conferences, bootcamps, and formal degrees. The direction they choose will depend on the skills they are trying to learn and their current level of expertise. This choice will have a direct impact on the length of time needed to attain proficiency and the cost. On one hand, books may provide the cheapest option but will rely on self-discipline and an independent learner. On the other hand, courses and bootcamps will cost more but will provide hands-on learning and an environment in which to ask questions. Ultimately, the investment in their learning should lead to meaningful contributions towards bringing the project to completion.

Though investment in your team will always be additive to the individual's skills and their resume, a quick word of caution before embarking on this journey: not all skills are valued equally. What do I mean by this? Well, based on the role (e.g., analytics) and scope (dashboarding, reporting, etc.), the skills you may be looking to train in (e.g., designing data architecture) may not be "in scope" and therefore not valued fully. Especially in larger companies, where your role and scope are well defined, take the time to understand whether the skills you are aiming to train for are "in scope" or not. If the answer is no, you'll need to consider where you can find teams or individuals for whom this is more appropriate. Alternatively, we suggest looking for an external specialist, which we will discuss more in the next section.

EXTERNAL RESOURCES

When the data skills are limited on your existing team, the opportunity cost of moving them off current projects is too high, or the trainable skills are outside of the scope of your team, you may search for external specialists (or generalists) to help. As a short-term fix, you will likely turn to contractors or consultants who can help fill the skill gap(s) and get the project running and on its feet. This allows your existing team members to focus on current, high-value, high-impact projects and simultaneously moves your project along—the best of both worlds! As a longer-term approach, you will want to find permanent hires that can help maintain, iterate, and improve anything you establish with short-term hires.

One of the most challenging hats you'll wear as the owner of this new deployment process will be that of a hiring manager. In most specialties, there are standardized tests that help gauge candidate competency. However, in data, there is no standard exam, test, or way to prove competency. It's a double-edged sword. From the employee's standpoint, the expectations of what to learn and maintain fluency in is vast, evolving, and challenging to keep up with. On the employer's side, resumes start to look the same, focused on expertise in the same tools and based on the same training exercises. Thus, resumes become limiting, and you must refer elsewhere to gauge current proficiency standards, exploring established portfolios online (GitHub, Kaggle, etc.), or you may need to take the time to formally interview candidates. Questions you might be interested in include: Can they demonstrate mastery of the program, tool, or language through a portfolio or their prior work? Does their existing experience lend itself to the tasks for which you are hiring? Does their project history align with the domain or industry you are in?

Beyond the tangible skills they can bring to the table on day one (Python, SQL, Tableau, etc.), how can you assess the intangible? It's true that there are hundreds of data courses and certifications, but none exists on the particular internal operations of your business. How can you assess the intellectual curiosity and creativity of the candidate, and how they will be able to apply their experience to your business? Ideally, a marriage of technicality and the aptitude to understand the business are core to successful hires.

Depending on the urgency of your need to hire talent, you might be pressed to pick the best out of the handful of candidates you had time to interview and move on. When that level of urgency doesn't exist, we like to be reminded of the theory of optimal stopping and the "37% rule," which can help you arrive at a decision faster. This rule essentially states to interview the first 37% of the candidate pool, choosing none, and then be ready to offer the position to the first candidate who is better than any you've interviewed so far. In either case, you may be rushed to a decision or be left with no option but to settle. You'll need to be wary of a bad hire, as the cost of onboarding and training for a new employee who ends up being a bad fit for the culture or role could be costly and put the project behind schedule.

When considering the longer-term vision for building your all-star team, you'll want to start thinking about full-time employees (FTEs), or permanent hires. Depending on the needs, you can look to hire specialists who can fill any skills gap or, alternatively, generalists who are keen to learn and eager to grow can supplement and enthuse an existing team. Additionally, hiring with diversity in mind can mean better business outcomes. Research clearly shows that diverse teams and companies show better business outcomes than their less diverse counterparts. For example, research by Fundera found that "racially and ethnically diverse companies are 35% more likely to perform better, while diverse teams are 70% more likely to capture and penetrate new markets."[1] Nowadays, most companies have specific diversity, equity, and inclusion (DEI) initiatives that help enforce this from the top, with sourcing sprints and training for hiring managers to help attract diverse candidates into the applicant pool. However, if your company doesn't have these practices in place, you can always work to be more intentional about your hiring practices—look to incorporate inclusive language in your requisitions and provide an inviting culture.

SETTING UP CAREER PATHWAYS

No matter which path you take to get things moving, leveraging your internal team or seeking external support, you will want to take a long-term approach to setting up your team for success. While your analytical products are the output, your team is the engine that keeps them running. So, take the time to set up relevant and exciting career paths for them so they will stay curious and motivated and grow in their careers. This way, you will have an easier time attracting good candidates and retaining strong talent on your team.

---

1 Thomas Helfrich, "How Diversity Can Help with Business Growth," *Forbes Magazine Council Post*, November 9, 2022, *https://oreil.ly/6fUl3*.

Although the typical track for those who work in corporate America is to start out as an individual contributor and then move up the chain to manage people and beyond, this is no longer the only option for individuals aiming to grow their careers. For analytics and general data roles, you will typically see two tracks set up: the *manager* and *principal* roles. Based on these tracks, get to know each individual on the team and what their career aspirations are, with these questions in the background: Are all great data scientists and analysts great leaders? Is a higher managerial position what they want? How can you create a career for your data specialists that means they are motivated, so you can retain them? Let's look at these two tracks in a bit more detail:

Tracks for managers

Team members on this track are typically eager for leadership and demonstrate an ability to take charge of large projects. Through project management, they likely indirectly manage other team members and demonstrate leadership. Training for individuals on this track could look like allowing for small opportunities for management through supervising interns. There are also many management training sessions that your team can invest in to learn things like DiSC styles, learning and communication styles, and general project management.

Tracks for principals

When team members have no desire to move along the route of people management, they typically like to have another way to grow and develop that doesn't restrict them to one career path. This is where moving towards a principal role comes into play. From a training and L&D perspective, your work will never be done here. The landscape continues to evolve—new technology, warehousing solutions, concepts, and frameworks are continually being developed to accommodate larger and larger data systems. Additionally, open source technology continues to improve, so newcomers and SMEs with limited analytics backgrounds can get up and running. The democratization of these tools has allowed a wider span of individuals, all across teams and levels of coding and statistical knowledge, to leverage powerful tools for their business use cases. It will be up to you to keep abreast of these tools and look for ways to test, foster learning, and find ways to leverage these tools within your team. Thus, your approach to learning and development for the team should continuously encourage independent learning through smaller projects, or a sandbox where ideas and tools can be tested. This will require team members with the skills necessary to run the new or improved systems you have set up for the team. This could be in the form of continued investment in L&D for the team, as mentioned, or bringing on new hires who can help fill skill gaps.

Defining the Right Structure for your Organization

How you structure your team will be an important, and nuanced, decision you will need to make. On one hand, you may choose to bring everyone together into one team (a centralized approach), and on the other, you may choose to align them directly as smaller groups, positioned more closely to the businesses they support (a decentralized approach). Let's talk about the pros and cons of each design structure.

CENTRALIZED VERSUS DECENTRALIZED

In a *centralized* support structure, as seen in Figure 5-1, your analytics team will exist as a separate entity in the organization, responsible for servicing all stakeholders through a central queue. One of the biggest benefits of this structure is that it allows all requests to come through you for prioritization before being delegated to for analysis. This can allow you time to understand, refine, and prioritize tasks based on business needs and desired impact. Additionally, you can consolidate tasks that are duplicative across multiple stakeholders, creating one reporting output that satisfies multiple needs. This leans in to principles like the 80/20 rule, which suggests that 20% of your effort will cover 80% of the tasks coming to the team. This is the philosophy that drives the engine of a centralized team, as they tackle big projects that can help accommodate the majority of use cases and needs across a business. There are many other benefits of this approach beyond prioritization, such as knowledge sharing, report standardization, and peer-to-peer mentorship. With centralized structures in place, your team will get exposure to a wide variety of business problems and form a strong team bond, which allows for much stronger collaboration.

The downsides to a centralized approach can come from lack of domain expertise as more complex team-specific tasks in the queue are assigned. Analysts taking on these tasks may be less familiar with the nuances of the metrics and the stakeholders, which will lead to time delays to get the output completed. Unfortunately, this can leave some teams with specific needs at a disadvantage, wherein they may have limited support, and at times may be flying blind. Circumventing this may be challenging due to competing priorities, but maintaining strong communication flows with all stakeholders regarding what the team is focused on, and when they can expect their needs to be met, could help calm the waters.

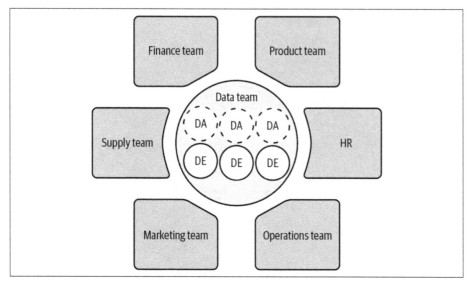

Figure 5-1. Centralized approach (adapted from an image by David Murray (https://oreil.ly/NwqYs))

In a *decentralized* approach, as seen in Figure 5-2, your team is integrated into business units within the organization. Analysts are aligned to business units and are immersed in their day-to-day workflows, metrics, reporting, and management. Their role will require them to handle the tasks coming out of their respective teams and allow them to focus on tailored and nuanced reporting that satisfies the needs of the business unit. Additionally, they can become thought partners with their stakeholders. The biggest advantage to this approach involves the "need for speed." By aligning your team to business units, they also function as domain experts and can more quickly turn around output as compared to teams using centralized approach.

Downsides to a decentralized structure involve the requirement for each team member to manage their prioritization of tasks within their business group. Depending on the individual/stakeholder relationship and the team members' comfort with pushing back, this can (at times) lead to feelings of being overwhelmed. Finally, when the team is distributed in this way, silos are naturally created, and there is less collaboration among team members. As a leader, you will likely want to accommodate this by creating forums and other means of knowledge sharing and collaboration.

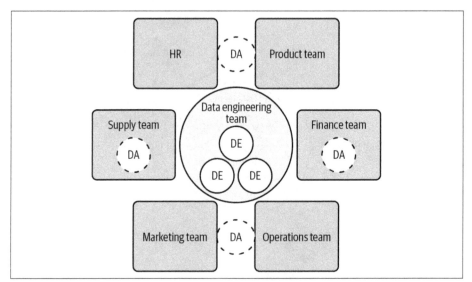

Figure 5-2. Decentralized approach (adapted from an image by David Murray (https://oreil.ly/Wh6kN))

THE HYBRID APPROACH

Centralized and decentralized approaches may feel like they fall on the extremes of the spectrum for designing your team structure, and that's because they are! So, if it feels like you're trying to fit a square peg into a round hole, you can turn to a hybrid approach. Hybrid approaches are more flexible and allow you to leverage the best features of both approaches while also tailoring it to you and your team's needs.

Though there are many options for how to construct a hybrid team, we will present one common option that we've personally encountered being leveraged in many companies. In this hybrid model, you will find team members aligned to departments or specific business functions (decentralized approach), all while being united under a group governing the standardization, output, and activity of the team (centralized approach). This allows for both the benefits of domain expertise and speed from the decentralized approach, and the standardization and knowledge sharing of the centralized approach, to be leveraged.

There will be other variations to consider about what type of hybrid approach to take, and you may lean more centralized or more decentralized. Luckily, there is no "one size fits all," and you should make the right decision for your team and your business needs, while also allowing yourself a sound framework to work within.

Establishing and Empowerment

The innovation and adoption of new data systems, approaches, reporting, and products in any company will rely heavily on the strength of the company's data culture. This culture usually starts at the top and trickles down. When the CEO and executive leadership have embraced a data culture, they will rally the team to this north star, helping root day-to-day strategy and decision-making in data and technology. But even in today's world, with technology and innovation moving at a never-before-seen pace, companies still face challenges with creating the right culture.

EXECUTIVE SPONSORSHIP

Since the onset of the boom in data and technology, every company has been faced with the choice of hopping onto the next fast-moving train or getting left behind. In the midst of these innovations and company shifts, there has been much research conducted to test the effectiveness and efficiency gains of becoming more data informed and prove the importance of culture to becoming more data informed. Overwhelming data and research points to all the benefits of becoming data informed or data led, as well as the rise of a new C-suite role—the chief data officer (CDO). However, the more challenging aspect is not just saying you want to become data informed but actually infusing that sentiment into the culture.[2]

> A NewVantage Partners survey of large U.S. firms, for example, found that only 31% of companies say they are data-driven, a figure that has declined from 37% in 2017. In 2019, more than three quarters reported that business adoption of big data and AI initiatives remains a major challenge. But 95% of them said that cultural, organizational, and process challenges presented the biggest roadblocks to adoption. Only 5% cited technology as the problem.

This points to the need to help leaders and CEOs feel more empowered with data. If there are gaps in leadership's understanding of data or tools, setting up the right operational partners and educational channels to help up-level the understanding of the implications of "getting left behind" or "moving too slowly" will be important to move this process along. They will need help in understanding the full scope of the changes, including the likely impacts on their products or services, the potential need for new skills to be developed through training or hiring, and the right organizational structure to support the company with more data. Once there is leadership buy-in and a lead-by-

---

2 Thomas H. Davenport and Nitin Mittal, "How CEOS Can Lead a Data-Driven Culture," *Harvard Business Review*, April 20, 2020, *https://oreil.ly/qFlJp*.

example mindset, the mission, narrative, and general culture will improve and help support how day-to-day tasks get executed and decisions get made.

Misalignment or a lack of buy-in from leadership makes it harder for certain teams to feel empowered, and projects, insights, or strategies can get stifled. Although it's easy for specific teams, like analytics and data science, to use and leverage data to drive insights and recommend strategy decisions, their influence is capped with limited leadership buy-in. When decisions need to be made and leadership shows little respect for what the data is showing or listens to data only when it confirms their ideology, that signals a weak reliance on data, and others will follow suit. Analysts and data science teams will continually have to raise awareness on data flaws, will struggle to get the right cross-functional support, and, in many cases, will not continue to get funded.

DATA-INFORMED CULTURE

Organizations that embrace strong data cultures generally maintain an openness to testing, learning, and iterating new data products developed by analytics, engineering, and data science teams. This has many advantages, as it helps build teams that work collaboratively to build new and improved processes and tools designed with automation and optimization in mind. It becomes easier to swap out outdated traditional approaches and work together to welcome new methodologies and iterate and improve them. Teams with strong data cultures have this ingrained in the mindset of each team member, as they are aiming for the same north star. This produces highly efficient and effective teams with strong levels of trust and higher-quality output. A nice by-product of a secure data-informed culture is the ability to move quickly and stay competitive in the market.

In teams or organizations with a weak data culture, you will find more hesitation to try new products and much longer iteration and adoption timelines. If you're operating in cultures like this, grit is your best friend. You will be moving against the grain and need to continue to sing the song of improved accuracy and improved processes, finding ways to incentivize use across the team. In cases where taking a bottom-up approach isn't working, you'll need to work your way to the top and find buy-in that can be enforceable through leadership support.

Unfortunately, the biggest headwind for building a strong and secure data culture is the fear and uncertainty around technology's fast advancement and its implication for job security. The answer to "will the technology I'm helping build work me out of a job?" is highly unknown—but the question lives within each of us. This can discourage team members from leaning in to product feedback that could threaten their jobs' existence. So how do we balance the need to innovate and embrace the world of data and technology without making team members feel a sense of insecurity? We can't fight the inevitable and risk becoming irrelevant or remaining inefficient—we should look to optimize and automate where possible. In a data-informed culture that is self-aware, leadership will ensure the message to the company is not to suggest removing people's jobs but to make them more efficient and find ways to repurpose employees to create more and more efficiency within the company's operations. It can be argued that automating mundane jobs that take hours or days of team members' time is time that can be repurposed somewhere else to benefit your organization's productivity.

As the rate of innovation around us continues, two schools of thought have begun to emerge: to embrace or to fight the change. Most recently, with the development of ChatGPT, we have seen questions around whether we are ready for this change and if we have developed the right policies to support the right innovation. In an open letter, 1,100+ signatories wrote:[3]

> Should we let machines flood our information channels with propaganda and untruth? Should we automate away all the jobs, including the fulfilling ones? Should we develop nonhuman minds that might eventually outnumber, outsmart, obsolete and replace us? Should we risk loss of control of our civilization? Such decisions must not be delegated to unelected tech leaders. Powerful AI systems should be developed only once we are confident that their effects will be positive and their risks will be manageable.

On the other hand, others would argue that we should be focused on how to better prepare for the changes to automation:[4]

> In a world where unemployment has become a stigma that sadly has impacted and still impacts millions of people, a title like this may seem like an unimaginable drama, but on the other side we can be sure that it will be a fulfilled prophecy, if we do nothing to be ready for this scenario. This possible scenario is the one we are headed, without brakes, and almost inexorably, at least if we assume that technological development will continue. The question is not if it will happen, but when and which country will be the first, maybe in decades, but with the current speed of change is more than probable that it will be technically "feasible" before mid-century.

The fundamentals stay the same no matter where you lie on this spectrum: an emphasis on data fluency and understanding the implications of whichever decision

---

3 Connie Loizos, "1,100+ Notable Signatories Just Signed an Open Letter Asking 'All AI Labs to Immediately Pause for at Least 6 Months,'" *TechCrunch*, March 29, 2023, *https://oreil.ly/hlCvy*.

4 David Vivancos, "The First Country with 100% Unemployment?" *LinkedIn*, August 30, 2022, *https://oreil.ly/RWBrk*.

you take. You will need to rally your team in that direction, and being clear on where you stand will help them understand your vision.

LIKELY CHALLENGES

Inevitably, you will face many challenges as you embark on this journey. Everything is on the table: balancing data needs with data costs, company pivots that require data pivots, earning leadership buy-in, finding the right talent, implementation challenges, and many, many more factors. As much as we've prepared you to think through all the important high-level considerations, there is no simple blueprint that will cover everything you may see or encounter.

The best qualities to carry with you are grit and adaptiveness. If you can maintain consistency in keeping the data narrative alive within your company, clearly articulating the "what needs to change" and the "why now," and adapting your approach as needed, then you will be set up for success. It's critical to remember that at the end of every change we make, whether it involves a process or a tool, is a human. It may be easy to make the decision to change a tool and implement it, but it takes people longer to change their mindsets, break habits, and learn new things. Thus, as a leader, it will be critical for you to lead with *empathy*.

What's Next?

First, thank you for taking the time to read this book. With your new knowledge, you should be feeling more confident to take on data-based projects. Keep in mind, though, that just having the knowledge won't necessarily make your next project a success. We recommend you take the following actions to improve your chances of making the changes your organization needs.

ENCOURAGE PROJECTS THAT CREATE A DATA-INFORMED ORGANIZATION

As a person of influence in your organization, you can help shape your company's path to becoming more data informed. When assessing what projects will move your team, department, or organization forward, ensure that there is data involved. Whether it is building a data source or a suite of analytical products or creating a new proposition from available data, you will be shaping your organization's attitudes towards data. The more data is used, the more everyone will feel motivated to use it.

FORM A DATA-FLUENT TEAM

Data products and propositions require that skilled specialists are involved in their build. If you have those skills in your organization already, identify who they are and foster their talents. When recruiting for roles in your organization, ensure data skills are part of the desired role profile alongside domain expertise and relevant experience. For those who are already in your organization but lack data skills, try to encourage the development of greater data fluency. If you have training budgets, ensure that courses are available to enhance your people's data fluency. Creating avenues for your team to take data courses and share knowledge is more likely to create greater resilience to changes in data use or any mistrust around the subject. Creating opportunities and highlighting the benefits of using data in the way your organization functions and makes decisions will change the culture for the better.

JUST GET STARTED

As much as it pains us to say, you'll never have the perfect data-fluent team receiving requests from data-informed executives right when the right data is readily available to answer those requests. The most important thing for you to do is to simply take steps towards creating the data-informed culture you've read about in this book. The more your organization uses data and the more trust that is built, the more data-informed decisions your company will make, enabling you to highlight the enhanced results from making more data-informed decisions.

There are many specialist books and resources available that address specific tools and the areas of data specialization that you will become involved with. We hope this book is just the beginning of your journey with data.

Index

Symbols

2-D position attribute, 47-48

3 Vs (big data), 3-4

A

access to data, 14-16

ad hoc analysis, 94

aggregation, 22-23, 36, 51

Agile development, 100-101

analytic tools, 89-91

analytical data sources, 35-37

analytical outputs, creating, 79-82

analytics platforms, building

    choosing architecture, 95-100

    deployment phase, 100-104

    developing business use cases, 104-106

    types of tools, 87-95

analyzing data sets, 54

APIs (Application Programming Interfaces), 62

Apple Watch, 33-34

audience

    approval from, 97

    for data projects, 82-86

automation, 104, 117

B

Beeline, 8, 85

best practices for visualizations, 46-50

BI (business intelligence) tools, 90

    dashboards, 42-45

    in data analysis, 81-82

    visualizations, 42

bias in data sets, 63

big bang migrations, 100

big data, 3-4

Boolean fields, 24-25

bottom-up approach (data observability), 103

building analytics platforms

    choosing architecture, 95-100

    deployment phase, 100-104

    developing business use cases, 104-106

    types of tools, 87-95

business use cases, developing, 104-106

C

Cambridge Analytica, 6

career pathways, 110-111

categories, 20

centralized organizational structure, 112-113

challenges, preparation for, 118

About the Authors

Carl Allchin is the head coach at one of the leading data training programs in the world. After nearly 10 years of working with data in financial services, Carl became a data consultant working across a vast range of industries before becoming a full-time trainer. When he started his career, Carl found the term *data* used dismissively but has been actively advocating for the broader adoption of data skills for all to allow everyone to make better decisions.

Sarah Nabelsi is a lifelong learner and data geek. Over the years, she has garnered a following as a personality on LinkedIn through her efforts to give back to the community—hosting meetups, blogging, presenting at conferences, and leading organizations like WiBD and GLAD. Her experience delivering innovative data tools, analysis, and models spans the entertainment, gaming, social media, and fintech spaces.

Colophon

The cover design and original cover art are by Susan Thompson. The cover fonts are Guardian Sans and Gilroy.